Writing the Critical Essay

Steroids

An **OPPOSING** **VIEWPOINTS®** Guide

Lauri S. Friedman, *Book Editor*

GREENHAVEN PRESS
A part of Gale, Cengage Learning

Detroit • New York • San Francisco • New Haven, Conn • Waterville, Maine • London

Christine Nasso, *Publisher*
Elizabeth Des Chenes, *Managing Editor*

© 2009 Greenhaven Press, a part of Gale, Cengage Learning

Gale and Greenhaven Press are registered trademarks used herein under license.

For more information, contact:
Greenhaven Press
27500 Drake Rd.
Farmington Hills, MI 48331-3535
Or you can visit our Internet site at gale.cengage.com

Articles in Greenhaven Press anthologies are often edited for length to meet page requirements. In addition, original titles of these works are changed to clearly present the main thesis and to explicitly indicate the author's opinion. Every effort is made to ensure that Greenhaven Press accurately reflects the original intent of the authors. Every effort has been made to trace the owners of copyrighted material.

Cover image Copyright Phil Date, 2008. Used Under license from Shutterstock.com.

LIBRARY OF CONGRESS CATALOGING-IN-PUBLICATION DATA

Steroids / Lauri S. Friedman, book editor.
   p. cm. — (Writing the critical essay, an opposing viewpoints guide)
  Includes bibliographical references and index.
  ISBN 978-0-7377-4267-1 (hardcover)
  1. Doping in sports. 2. Steroids. I. Friedman, Lauri S.
  RC1230.S7314 2009
  362.29—dc22

                                                2008028520

Printed in the United States of America
1 2 3 4 5 6 7 12 11 10 09 08

CONTENTS

Examining the state of writing and how it is taught in the United States was the official purpose of the National Commission on Writing in America's Schools and Colleges. The commission, made up of teachers, school administrators, business leaders, and college and university presidents, released its first report in 2003. "Despite the best efforts of many educators," commissioners argued, "writing has not received the full attention it deserves." Among the findings of the commission was that most fourth-grade students spent less than three hours a week writing, that three-quarters of high school seniors never receive a writing assignment in their history or social studies classes, and that more than 50 percent of first-year students in college have problems writing error-free papers. The commission called for a "cultural sea change" that would increase the emphasis on writing for both elementary and secondary schools. These conclusions have made some educators realize that writing must be emphasized in the curriculum. As colleges are demanding an ever-higher level of writing proficiency from incoming students, schools must respond by making students more competent writers. In response to these concerns, the SAT, an influential standardized test used for college admissions, required an essay for the first time in 2005.

Books in the Writing the Critical Essay: An Opposing Viewpoints Guide series use the patented Opposing Viewpoints format to help students learn to organize ideas and arguments and to write essays using common critical writing techniques. Each book in the series focuses on a particular type of essay writing—including expository, persuasive, descriptive, and narrative—that students learn while being taught both the five-paragraph essay as well as longer pieces of writing that have an opinionated focus. These guides include everything necessary to help students research, outline, draft, edit, and ultimately write successful essays across the curriculum, including essays for the SAT.

Using Opposing Viewpoints

This series is inspired by and builds upon Greenhaven Press's acclaimed Opposing Viewpoints series. As in the parent series, each book in the Writing the Critical Essay series focuses on a timely and controversial social issue that provides lots of opportunities for creating thought-provoking essays. The first section of each volume begins with a brief introductory essay that provides context for the opposing viewpoints that follow. These articles are chosen for their accessibility and clearly stated views. The thesis of each article is made explicit in the article's title and is accentuated by its pairing with an opposing or alternative view. These essays are both models of persuasive writing techniques and valuable research material that students can mine to write their own informed essays. Guided reading and discussion questions help lead students to key ideas and writing techniques presented in the selections.

The second section of each book begins with a preface discussing the format of the essays and examining characteristics of the featured essay type. Model five-paragraph and longer essays then demonstrate that essay type. The essays are annotated so that key writing elements and techniques are pointed out to the student. Sequential, step-by-step exercises help students construct and refine thesis statements; organize material into outlines; analyze and try out writing techniques; write transitions, introductions, and conclusions; and incorporate quotations and other researched material. Ultimately, students construct their own compositions using the designated essay type.

The third section of each volume provides additional research material and writing prompts to help the student. Additional facts about the topic of the book serve as a convenient source of supporting material for essays. Other features help students go beyond the book for their research. Like other Greenhaven Press books, each book in the Writing the Critical Essay series includes bibliographic listings of relevant periodical articles, books, Web sites, and organizations to contact.

Writing the Critical Essay: An Opposing Viewpoints Guide will help students master essay techniques that can be used in any discipline.

Steroids: Useful Tool or Shameful Shortcut?

The use and abuse of steroids in sports is not a new problem: beginning in the 1930s when the class of drugs known as anabolic steroids was discovered by scientists, steroids were used by bodybuilders and weight lifters to gain an edge over their competition. The use of steroids in sport has since continued to be debated, coming to a head in recent years when a steroids scandal rocked the world of major league baseball. Steroids use raises many fascinating questions about fairness in sport, such as the debate over what constitutes an unfair advantage in an athletic competition.

Steroid use is primarily frowned upon because many people view drug use as a shortcut to athletic prowess; an athlete who breaks a world record because he was pumped up on steroids, for example, garners less respect and honor than one who did it with natural talent, innate skill, and hard work. George W. Bush articulated this sentiment in 2004 when he called upon the nation's teachers, coaches, parents, and sports fans to reject the use of steroids in athletics. Said the president: "The use of performance-enhancing drugs like steroids in baseball, football, and other sports is dangerous, and it sends the wrong message—that there are shortcuts to accomplishment, and that performance is more important than character."[1] For Bush and many others, athletes who use steroids taint not only their sport, but their personal honor.

But not everyone believes that the use of performance-enhancing drugs undermines the true spirit of sports—in fact, it is often argued that steroids are just one of many tools used by athletes to perform their best. Indeed, some claim that steroids are no different than other performance-enhancing products available to modern athletes, such as

In 2004 President George W. Bush called upon the nation's teachers, coaches, parents, players, and fans to reject the use of steroids.

ergonomic swimwear, high-tech sneakers, and aerodynamic clothing. "Not all shortcuts come in pills or capsules," argues writer Jacob Sullum. "An athlete who uses the latest exercise equipment, fitness knowledge, and nutritional expertise to get into shape is using shortcuts that were unavailable to his predecessors 30 or 40 years ago."[2] Columnist Eugene Robinson agrees—he points out that golfer Tiger Woods improved his vision by getting laser surgery, and asks, "Have any major leaguers with normal vision gone under the laser in an attempt to gain an edge? Wouldn't submitting healthy eyes to a performance-enhancing operation be just as problematic as taking steroids or growth hormones?"[3] What these and other commentators argue is that contemporary athletic competitions are not about who has the best skills anyway, but about who has the best access to cutting-edge trainers, procedures, and equipment.

Still others bristle at the notion that athletes who take steroids are shortcutting at all and reject the suggestion that such athletes do not work as hard as "clean" athletes. Journalist Adrianne Blue explains that taking steroids does not automatically make someone a better athlete—it merely gives them opportunities to train longer and harder. "What many of us don't realize is that sports doping rarely gives you a free ride," says Blue. "If you or I were to take anabolic steroids and sit down in front of the telly [television], we would not build muscle or speed or endurance."[4] Indeed, drugs like steroids allow an athlete to recover from injury more quickly, train longer, and get more out of weight training sessions—but they do not do the work for the athlete.

But just knowing that players have used steroids ruins the pleasure of watching a game for many sports fans, who claim that physical achievements that result from chemicals detract from what sport is supposed to be about in the first place: the raw power of the human body. As George J. Mitchell wrote in his infamous Mitchell Report, which exposed a major steroids scandal in major league baseball, "The illegal use of performance enhancing substances poses a serious threat to the integrity of the game. Widespread use by players of such substances unfairly disadvantages the honest athletes who refuse to use them and raises questions about the validity of baseball records."[5] It appears that the majority of the American public agrees with Mitchell that steroid use compromises the integrity of sports: This is why 62 percent of Americans told pollsters from ABC News and ESPN that they think players should be forced to lose their records if they have been discovered to use steroids, and 66 percent want athletes who have used steroids to be banned from the Hall of Fame.

Yet others claim that steroid use does not detract from a game—in fact, for some, the use of steroids by players actually enhances the quality and excitement of an athletic event. Sullum compares an athlete who takes steroids to perform his best with an actress who gets breast implants or cosmetic surgery to look her best on camera. "And just as it is possible to enjoy an actress's performance despite her artificial enhancements," he writes, "it should be possible to enjoy a football or baseball game despite the use of steroids or stimulants—and obviously it is, since fan interest in these sports has not exactly evaporated in recent years, despite periodic doping scandals."[6] Put another way, Eugene Robinson has suggested that Americans like their athletes faster, bigger,

Sixty-two percent of Americans believe players should lose their records if they have used steroids to enhance their performance.

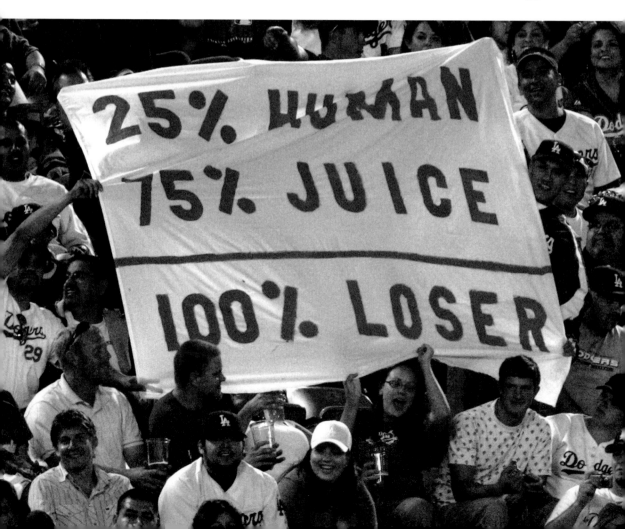

and capable of more—it makes for a more thrilling game, which is what ultimately sells tickets. "We, the paying customers, don't want normal-size athletes with normal abilities," argues Robinson. "We want to see supermen and superwomen performing super feats, and we're willing to pay these gladiators a fortune. Why should they disappoint us? Why should we expect them to?"[7]

Whether steroid use undermines the true nature of sport is just one of the topics explored in *Writing the Critical Essay: An Opposing Viewpoints Guide: Steroids*. Whether steroids should be legal, whether their use constitutes cheating, and whether student athletes should have to submit to mandatory steroids testing are all explored in passionately argued essays by reputable sources. Model essays and thought-provoking writing exercises help readers develop their own opinions and write their own descriptive essays on this compelling and multifaceted subject.

Notes

1. George W. Bush, "State of the Union Address," January 20, 2004. www.whitehouse.gov/news/releases/2004/ 01/20040120-7.html. Accessed May 9, 2008.
2. Jacob Sullum, "Bush on Steroids: Why Must Sports Be Drug-Free?" *Reason*, January 23, 2004. www.reason.com/ news/show/35605.html.
3. Eugene Robinson, "Fans on the Juice," *Washington Post*, December 18, 2007. www.washingtonpost.com/wpdyn/ content/article/2007/12/17/AR2007121701597.html.
4. Adrianne Blue, "It's the Real Dope," *New Statesman*, August 14, 2006.
5. George J. Mitchell, "Report to the Commissioner of Baseball of an Independent Investigation into the Illegal Use of Steroids and Other Performance Enhancing Substances by Players in Major League Baseball," December 13, 2007. http://files.mlb.com/summary.pdf.
6. Sullum, "Bush on Steroids."
7. Robinson, "Fans on the Juice."

Section One: Opposing Viewpoints on Steroids

Steroids Should Be Legal

Oakland Tribune

The following essay was written by editors at the *Oakland Tribune*, a newspaper serving the San Francisco Bay Area. The authors suggest making performance-enhancing drugs legal as a way of dealing with the problem of steroid use in sports. Since fans expect professional athletes to continually break records and outperform each other, the authors suggest it is unlikely that professional athletes will be able to stop using steroids any time soon. But if steroids were legal, their use could be monitored and controlled by a team of doctors who would make sure athletes used the drugs safely. Furthermore, the millions that are wasted on trying to curb the use of illegal drugs could be spent more wisely. The authors conclude that keeping steroids illegal forces athletes to use them in dangerous secrecy: Legalizing them would bring the issue out in the open where it could be dealt with safely and profitably.

Consider the following questions:

1. What aspect of professional sports do the authors think is insulting to fans' intelligence?
2. What connection do the authors make between steroid use and the prohibition of alcohol?
3. What cruel and unusual choice are professional athletes forced to make, in the authors' opinion?

$\mathbf{T}$ime to call the doctor.

Heck, dial several of them. In the wake of M-Day—the landmark Thursday in which former Senate Majority Leader George Mitchell dumped baseball's tawdriness on

Former senator George Mitchell oversaw the congressional investigation of illegal steroids in Major League Baseball.

the public like so much dirty laundry[1]—the sport really doesn't have any other choice.

It's time for Major League Baseball (MLB) to consider making performance-enhancing drugs a welcome, and legal, part of its culture.

Stop Forcing Athletes to Lie

Lunacy? Perhaps, but no more so than the notion of a 36-year-old pitcher on the downside of his career winning 14 consecutive decisions out of the blue without help. Well, maybe Roger Clemens believes that's what happened in 1998, but after reading the Mitchell Report, the rational among us no longer do.

1. The author is referring to the Mitchell Report, which exposed the widespread use of steroids in baseball.

Of course, Clemens is in the same mode that has infected almost every modern athlete with smoke attached to this fire. Deny, deny, deny. Then throw in the requisite, "I passed every drug test."

Honestly, isn't that so insulting to the intelligence that it makes you want to toss your lunch? All of which, if nothing else, speaks to the cultural ill that exists in the disgraced old game, and the disconnect it has with reality. Commissioner Bud Selig has been prone to stand on his soap box over the years and preach that the game has never been healthier, and the players never more popular. And judging by the financial books, it's been a pretty good argument.

The Mitchell Report changed that. Yes, there are holes in it, but the one thing it proves beyond a reasonable doubt is this: Baseball has never been more sick, and its players never more shady.

Legalizing Steroids Allows Them to Be Regulated

And this is where doctors would enter the picture. And why some serious consideration should be given to this idea. You see, juice will be exterminated from the game about the time universal health care is adopted. The use of performance-enhancing drugs is a run-away fire, and the testers are the firemen desperately trying to catch up. The magic of baseball's numbers are gone.

So why not take a new approach? Why not take some of that record $6.2 billion in revenue that the sport generated a season ago and establish a central medical office, one that's staffed with the leading experts in the performance-enhancing area that can be made available for players from the majors to high school. After

Athletes Should Use Steroids Under Doctor's Supervision

Legal restrictions and league bans on steroids discourage athletes who use them from seeking medical guidance, so they're more at risk than they would be if steroid use were permitted. As with recreational drugs, prohibition makes steroids *more* dangerous, not less.

Jacob Sullum, "Bush on Steroids: Why Must Sports Be Drug-Free?" *Reason*, January 23, 2004. www.reason.com/news/show/35605.html.

Roger Clemens, right, accused of steroid use, testifies before George Mitchell's congressional committee investigating his alleged steroid use.

all, investing it in an independent drug-testing organization wouldn't be a cure-all; such an approach by the International Olympic Committee hasn't steered its athletes free of controversy.

Why not take some more of that money and pass it on to some lobbyists on Capitol Hill? Argue to those grandstanding congressmen that the juicing of players can't be policed, not when the code of the clubhouse is even more impenetrable than that of the Mafia.

Drugs Are a Part of Our Culture

Heck, argue that performance enhancers have become necessary. Seasons start in mid-February and can run as long as early November. Fewer doubleheaders mean far fewer days off. A team can play one game at night on the East Coast, then play early the next evening on the West Coast.

In other words, the body is subject to punishment that didn't exist 30 years ago. And this doesn't even take into account the grueling nature of football, hoops and all the other big-time sports, none of which should be discounted, because doping is a professional sports problem, not just a baseball one.

So it is then that it's time, at the very least, for some discussion about an idea that's as radical as the repealing of prohibition once was. And while the juice should not be as easily attainable as alcohol—make it available only by a prescription from an MLB doctor at the central office with no puny deductible—why shouldn't it be available for those who decide it's worth the cost? As for what that might be, only the experts would know.

Keep this in mind, however. A culture schooled in the convenience of remote controls and online shopping will need far more than some salacious name-dropping to change its spending habits.

Keep this in mind, also: The availability of such everyday drugs as Viagra—now there's a performance enhancer—is everywhere, and we keep flocking to them despite the paragraph's worth of risks with which they're usually associated.

A Cruel and Unusual Choice

It would seem that the greater hazard would be to allow baseball to keep on keepin' on, enabling a culture that forces their players to prove their innocence and causes our athletic sons and daughters to make a choice—follow the cheaters or go through the back alleys to keep up—that seems cruel and unusual.

So please, everybody to the table and start discussing it. Maybe the idea is out of the box, but at least it's not status quo. That, after all, would be the greatest danger of all.

Analyze the essay:

1. The authors argue that since it is impossible to stop athletes from taking steroids, their use should be made legal so it can be monitored and controlled. What main assumption is made in order for the argument to hold up?

2. The authors suggest that making steroids legal can protect athletes and save money on useless policing efforts. This suggestion—that a substance or procedure should be legalized in order to make it safer—is frequently made when people debate other controversial topics, such as abortion, alcohol, and marijuana. In your opinion, is legalizing something to make it safer a valid course of action? Why or why not?

Steroids Should Be Illegal

Donald M. Hooton

In the following essay Donald M. Hooton argues that steroids are dangerous and should be illegal. He describes athletes who use steroids as cheaters and cowards and laments that their behavior is emulated by so many young people. One such person was Hooton's son, Taylor, whose death in 2003 was related to his secret steroid use. Hooton says that baseball players who use steroids must realize that young people are dying in their pursuit to be like their favorite athletes. He also says that coaches, parents, and teachers must work harder to make sure steroids have no place on high school or professional sports teams. Hooton concludes that steroid use is a major problem, and their use should be discouraged in professional and amateur sports.

Donald M. Hooton is the father of Taylor Hooton, who killed himself on July 15, 2003. It is believed that Taylor's steroid use made him prone to severe depression, which led him to commit suicide. After his son's death, Hooton founded the Taylor Hooton Foundation, a nonprofit organization dedicated to fighting steroid use.

Consider the following questions:

1. What percent of high school students use steroids, according to Hooton?
2. What message does Hooton say steroid-using professional athletes send to kids?
3. What consequences should an athlete who uses steroids face, in Hooton's opinion?

Donald M. Hooton, "Oral Testimony," House Government Reform Committee, www.taylorhooton.org, March 17, 2005. Reproduced by permission of the author.

Twenty short months ago, our youngest son Taylor took his own life. He was just 2 weeks away from beginning his senior year in high school. He was carrying a 3.8 average, had made an excellent score on his SAT test, and we were preparing to make college visits. Taylor was well liked by all who knew him—adults tell us he was one of the most well mannered young men that they ever met—he was always smiling! His friends tell us that he was one of the nicest kids on campus, a ladies man who was a real charmer.

This past spring, he would have been a starting pitcher on his varsity baseball team. During the fall of his junior year, his JV coach told this 6'3"/175 pound young man that he needed to "get bigger" to improve his chances of making varsity. Taylor resorted to using anabolic steroids as a short cut to reach his objective.

Recent studies have shown that five to six percent of U.S. high school athletes are using steroids.

I am convinced that Taylor's secret use of anabolic steroids played a significant role in causing the severe depression that resulted in his suicide. I have learned that what happened to Taylor—the events leading up to and including his suicide—are right out of the medical textbook on steroids.

America's High School Steroid Problem

Experts put the steroid usage rate at about 5–6% of the total US High School population—about a million kids. I am convinced that those numbers understate the problem. Some studies have put the use of steroids at about 11–12% of the junior/senior high male school population in some parts of the country. To put these numbers into perspective, the kids I've spoken with estimate that at least a third of the high school players that show up to play football under the lights on Friday nights in my part of the country are "juicing."

A number of factors are contributing to the increase in steroid usage amongst our kids—you have invited me to discuss one of them.

I believe the poor example being set by professional athletes is a major catalyst fueling the high usage of steroids amongst our kids. Our kids look up to these guys—they want to do those things that the pros do to be successful. With this in mind, I have some messages for the players:

Emulating Their Favorite Role Models

First, I am tired of hearing you tell us that kids should not look up to you as role models. If you haven't figured it out yet, let me break the news to you, you are role models whether you like it or not. And parents across America should hold you accountable for behavior that inspires our kids to do things that put their health at risk and teaches them that the ethics we try to teach them at home somehow don't apply to you.

Second, our kids know that the use of steroids is high amongst professional athletes. They don't need to read Mr. Canseco's new book to know that something other than natural physical ability is providing many of you with the ability to break so many performance records that provide you the opportunity to earn those millions of dollars.

With respect to the sacred home run record, I think Reggie Jackson's comments on this subject are instructional: "Somebody is definitely guilty of taking steroids. You can't break records hitting 200 home runs in 3 or 4 seasons. The greatest hitters in the history of the game didn't do that. Henry Aaron never hit 50 in a season, so you're going to tell me that you're a greater hitter than Henry Aaron? Bonds hit 73 in 2001, and he would have hit 100 if they had pitched to him. I mean, come on now."

Our youngsters hear the message: it's loud, it's clear, and it's wrong—"if you want to achieve your goals, it is okay to use steroids to get you there because the pros are doing it." It is a real challenge for today's parents to overpower the strong messages being sent to our kids by your behavior.

Steroids Turn Athletes into Cheaters and Cowards

Third, players that are guilty of taking steroids are not only cheaters but you are also cowards. You are afraid to step onto the field, compete for your positions, and play the game without the aid of substances that are a felony to possess without a legitimate prescription; substances that have been banned from competition at all levels of athletics.

Steroids Are Dangerous

Steroids cause many adverse short- and long-term side effects in boys, men, and women. For this reason many people consider them to be too dangerous to legalize.

Short-Term Adverse Effects of Steroids in Boys

- Early sexual development
- Penis enlargement
- Painful, prolonged penile erections
- Premature closure of the growth plates in long bones resulting in a decrease in the total height achieved
- Fluid retention, swelling

Short-Term Adverse Effects of Steroids in Men

- Acne
- Skin tissue damage at the site of injection
- Shrinking of the testicles
- Decreased sperm production and motility
- Decreased semen volume
- Frequent or continuing erections
- Enlargement of the breast (gynecomastia)
- Elevated blood pressure
- Increased LDL cholesterol levels
- Decreased HDL cholesterol levels
- Fluid retention and swelling
- Abnormal liver function
- Prostate enlargement
- Bleeding (usually from the nose)

Short-Term Adverse Effects of Steroids in Women

- Acne
- Oily skin
- Tissue damage at injection site
- Deepening of the voice
- Increased body and facial hair growth
- Enlargement of the clitoris
- Male pattern baldness
- Decreased breast size
- Menstrual irregularities (missed periods or no periods)
- Fluid retention and swelling

Long-Term Consequences of Steroid Abuse in Men and Women

- Liver dysfunction
- Liver tumors
- Liver cancer
- Prostate cancer (men only)
- Increased blood pressure
- Enlargement of the heart
- Death of heart cells
- Heart attacks
- Stroke

Taken from: James Tolliver, Drug Enforcement Administration, Drug and Chemical Evaluation Section.

Not only that, you are cowards when it comes to facing your fans and the kids. Why don't you behave like we try to teach our kids to behave? Show our kids that you are man enough to face authority, tell the truth, and face the consequences. Instead, you hide behind the skirts of your union and now, with the help of management and your lawyers, you have made every effort to resist facing the public today. What message are you sending our sons and daughters? That you are above the law? That you can continue to lie, deny your behavior, and get away with it? That somehow you are not a cheater unless you get caught? . . .

Major League Baseball Must Get Rid of Steroids

Now, a message for management: Major League Baseball and other sports need to take serious steps to stop the use of steroids. Slapping a player on the wrist with a 10-day suspension sends just one more signal to the kids that you are not serious about ridding the game of this junk. Forcing a pro to miss just 6% of the season is equivalent to forcing a high school kid to sit the bench for less than one of his games! And, we shouldn't be talking about whether to put an asterisk next to these guys' records! We're missing the whole point. You should be throwing them out of the big leagues.

Why don't you implement a real program that's closer to the Olympic program where cheaters are unable to compete for two years after their first offense and banned for life following their second? Do that and the kids may begin to get the impression that you are taking this issue seriously! . . .

Making Teams Steroid-Free

Students need to understand that these drugs can seriously harm them. But warning a 16-year-old about the dangers of having a heart attack or developing liver problems when he is 35 or 40 will probably fall on deaf ears.

That's why I believe that parents and coaches are our most important targets for education. Parents need to know the dangers of this drug, how to recognize warning signs, and understand the importance of supervising their children in this area.

Our coaches must be more responsible and accountable for supervising this situation with their teams. Coaches across the country need to be:

a) Certified and credentialed—to have to pass a test to prove they are competent to supervise our kids. As part of their certification, they need to be trained to recognize the symptoms of steroid and other performance enhancing drug abuse and trained to know what to do about it when they find it, and

Barry Bonds' record-breaking 756th home run has been tainted by Bonds' alleged steroid use.

b) Held accountable for insuring that their teams are steroid-free. They should enforce a true zero tolerance policy against steroid abuse. . . .

On behalf of Taylor Hooton, Rob Garibaldi, Efrain Marrero and other kids around the country who have lost their lives to steroids, let me implore you to take steps to clean this mess up. Please help us to see that our children's lives were not lost in vain. You have the power to do something about this problem, and we are counting on you to do so.

Analyze the essay:

1. In this essay Donald M. Hooton uses descriptive techniques to paint a picture of his son, Taylor, who died from steroid use. What did you learn about Taylor? What kind of student was he? What other details did you learn about his life? Did learning these details make you more sympathetic to Hooton's argument? Explain your reasoning.

2. Hooton uses the death of his son as an example of why steroids should be illegal. How do you think the authors of the previous essay by the *Oakland Tribune* might respond to this suggestion and the circumstances surrounding Taylor's death?

Steroid Use Makes Sports Unfair

Douglas R. Hochstetler

In the following essay Douglas R. Hochstetler argues that the use of steroids constitutes cheating in sports. He considers various methods used by athletes to gain the competitive advantage—methods that range from hard work, special training, moves and techniques, and drug use. He says that sports fans respect athletes who combine biological gifts with hard work to achieve athletic success, not those who use unfair training techniques or get help from drugs and chemicals. The author concludes that while sports can reflect some of humanity's best characteristics (sportsmanship, determination, and teamwork), they can also represent its worst (greed, underhandedness, and cheating). He urges athletes, coaches, and fans to keep athletics fair and honorable by frowning upon steroid use in sports.

Hochstetler is associate professor of kinesiology at Penn State University, Lehigh Valley campus, where he teaches a course on ethics in sports.

Consider the following questions:

1. Who is Rex Ryan, and what is his view about the purpose of sports, as reported by the author?
2. What three socially constructed conventions does Hochstetler compare sports to?
3. Why is it necessary, in Hochstetler's opinion, to clarify why Americans value competition?

I teach a number of courses at Penn State, one of which focuses on sport ethics. My students never need to look far, unfortunately, for examples of unethical acts and attitudes in sport. Take your pick from the following list: Barry Bonds (alleged) and Marion Jones (confessed) connection to steroid use, the Tour de France doping scandals, and New England Patriots Coach Bill Belichick and "Spygate."[1]

When these events occur, people respond in a number of ways. Some condemn the incident but continue to support the athlete, coach or team. Others point out a perceived decline in ethical behavior in sport and society. Still more decry the misplaced emphasis on sport and athletics in the first place. The cynics even contend that sport ethics is an oxymoron—that to compete at high levels requires at minimum a bit of cheating. If one believes sport has at least the possibility of displaying, and even encouraging, ethical behavior, then perhaps we might learn from these recent unethical events.

> **Steroids Violate the Spirit of the Game**
>
> The illegal use of performance enhancing substances poses a serious threat to the integrity of the game. Widespread use by players of such substances unfairly disadvantages the honest athletes who refuse to use them and raises questions about the validity of baseball records.
>
> George J. Mitchell, "Report to the Commissioner of Baseball of an Independent Investigation into the Illegal Use of Steroids and Other Performance Enhancing Substances by Players in Major League Baseball," December 13, 2007. http://files.mlb.com/summary.pdf.

The Heart of Sports

Following the Patriots' incident, Rex Ryan, defensive coordinator for the Baltimore Ravens said, "I'm not sure sports are supposed to be about who can cheat the best." This is precisely the issue the NFL and other sport organizations need to address. What should competitive sport be about in the first place? What is at the heart of our interscholastic, intercollegiate, and elite athletic programs? Why do we (both fans and participants) value

1. The author is referring to a 2007 scandal in which a National Football League team was accused of videotaping another team's signals.

them? Rather than simply bemoaning the fact that these incidents occur, we could view them as the motive for reflection on the nature of sport.

To a large degree, sport involves the contesting of superior skills. In the case of the NFL, we follow these competitions in part to see which teams and individuals display better blocking, tackling, passing, receiving, defending skills, and so forth. Many sports allow both individual athletes and teams to show brilliance when it comes to strategy as well. Football fans appreciate when the defensive coordinator develops a brilliant game plan

Baltimore Ravens' coach Rex Ryan has commented that sports should not be about "who can cheat the best." Statements like this have brought more attention to the topic of steroid use in professional sports.

Steroids Corrupt the Game

The majority of Americans believe steroid use constitutes cheating, according to a joint ABC/ESPN poll. As a result, they believe athletes who are caught using drugs should have their records deleted and be banned from the Hall of Fame.

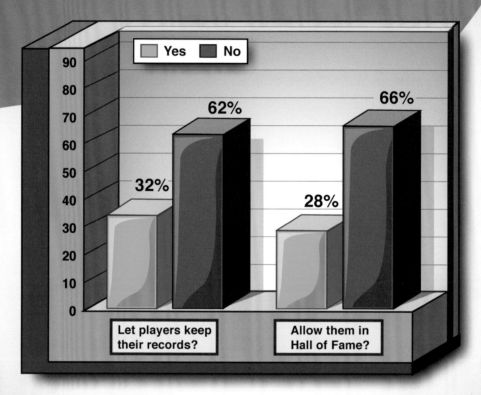

Taken from: ABC News/ESPN poll: Steroids and Baseball, March 15, 2005.

to stifle the opposition's offense. Likewise, baseball fans value a timely pitching change, double-steal, or defensive substitution.

We Respect Human Achievements, Not Enhanced Ones

However, we value superior skills honed in a certain way—through what political philosopher Michael Sandel terms "giftedness." This means athletic skills cultivated as a result of biological assets in combination with effort and hard work. In short, we respect athletes who display human—not technologically aided, genetically enhanced or steroid-driven—capabilities. We want to see which

Occasionally athletes and coaches skirt ethical boundaries to achieve success, as was the case with New England Patriots coach Bill Belichick and the "spygate" scandal.

team has the best athletes and not the best engineers, geneticists or chemists.

At times, athletes and coaches try to gain the upper hand by using methods that skirt the ethical boundaries. In fact, one might say that cheating involves skill, precision, and perhaps even practice. Occasionally, coaches and athletes use actions which could be considered cheating—such as flopping in basketball or taking a dive in soccer. For the Patriots, this technologically involved a video camera.

Keeping Sports Pure and Ethical

Sports are socially-constructed conventions similar to education, government, and the military. We shape athletics to fit our societal expectations, at times with pure motives but on other occasions suspect. Football, baseball, track and field, cycling and other sports can represent the finest qualities of humanity. Conversely, they can deteriorate into humans at their worst.

Sport organizations, from youth leagues to elite levels, need to remain vigilant with regards to their rules as well as the overall moral climate. Ethical decision-making is not easy. Questions such as, "How much performance enhancement should we allow?" is but one example of difficult and ongoing issues faced by sport communities. Thinking more carefully about the purpose of sport puts us in a better position to make these decisions however.

Steroid Use Constitutes Cheating

In the end, we all have a collective tendency for moral callousness—to rationalize our behavior because "everyone else is doing it," or "it's not cheating if I don't get caught." In this sense, the broader culture is not drastically different from the sport world. I hope these unethical sporting acts prompt discussions about the overall value of competition and sports. Perhaps, by clarifying why we value competition in the first place, we can discourage and prevent unethical acts in the future. Then, perhaps, my Penn State students will find it easier to find moral exemplars rather than miscreants in sport.

Analyze the essay:

1. Douglas R. Hochstetler is a kinesiologist, a person who deals with issues related to sports, recreation, and exercise. He also teaches a university-level course on ethics in sports. Does knowing his professional background influence the credence you give to his argument? Why or why not?

2. In making his point that steroid use is unfair, Hochstetler poses the question, "How much performance enhancement should be allowed?" What does he mean by this question? Write one paragraph about what he is getting at and what your answer to his question would be.

Steroid Use Makes Sports More Fair

Michael Le Page

In the following essay Michael Le Page argues that steroid use would level the playing field in sports. He considers what makes certain athletes so good at their sport—some have genetic mutations that make them unusually tall or make their blood advantageously rich in oxygen. Others have extraordinarily large or small body parts that give them the competitive advantage. Le Page says that with so many natural variations among athletes, there is no such thing as "fairness" in sport. With that being the case, he suggests that athletes be allowed to take performance-enhancing drugs to close the gap. Because steroids are illegal, athletes risk their health and even death when they use drugs unsupervised. Le Page suggests allowing medical experts to supervise steroid use so that athletes could be safe when using them. Le Page concludes that it makes no difference whether athletes succeed because they are advantaged biologically or chemically, just as long as they compete on an equal footing.

Le Page is a writer for *New Scientist*, from which this essay was taken.

Consider the following questions:

1. What gene mutation does Eero Mantyranta have, and how does it affect his athletic performance, according to Le Page?
2. What does Le Page say gives swimmer Ian Thorpe an advantage over his competitors?
3. What does the author mean when he says it is acceptable for athletes to risk "natural death" in competition?

Michael Le Page, "Only Drugs Can Stop the Sports Cheats," *New Scientist*, vol. 191, August 19, 2006, pp. 18–19. Copyright © 2006 Reed Elsevier Business Publishing, Ltd. Reproduced by permission.

The Finnish cross-country skier Eero Mantyranta won two gold medals in the 1964 Olympics and accumulated an impressive tally of medals during his career. Later it turned out that he has a mutation in a gene called FPOK that means he produces up to 50 per cent more red blood cells than normal.

The east African runners who dominate distance events have also been shown to have at least one genetic advantage: their lower legs are thinner and weigh on average 400 grams less than those of Danish athletes, which translates into a massive 8 per cent energy saving. Other people have distinct genetic disadvantages. For instance, 1 in 5 Europeans cannot produce the alpha-actinin-3 protein found in fast-twitch muscle fibres. Very few people with this genotype excel at power sports such as sprinting.

So much for fairness in sport. The World Anti-Doping Agency says its aim is "to protect the athletes' fundamental right to participate in doping-free sport and thus promote health, fairness, and equality for athletes worldwide". Such notions are a quaint hangover from the amateur age. Sports are inherently unfair. Genes alone do not make you a winner, of course, but some people's genes give them a massive advantage with which others struggle to compete no matter how young they start or how hard they train.

Performance-Enhancing Drugs Level the Playing Field

There is a way to level the paying field: allow athletes to make up for their natural disadvantages by taking performance-enhancing drugs. There is not yet a "foot growth potion" for the rivals of Australian swimmer Ian Thorpe, who has size-17 feet, but an estimated 1 million Americans have already taken human growth hormone, which in the US can now be prescribed for children with "idiopathic short stature"—effectively anyone who is very short. No one knows how many average-size people have used growth hormone to help them make the national basketball team, but would it really be fair to exclude such people as cheats when, for example, players such as Pavel Podkolzin or Sun Ming Ming owe their great height to pituitary tumours that resulted in an excess of growth hormone?

Basketball player Sun Ming Ming is very tall due to a pituitary tumor that gives him extra growth hormones. Some consider this to be an unfair athletic advantage.

Or take the mutation that boosted Mantyranta's red blood cell count. All athletes know that there are ways of equalling or surpassing his natural advantage: take the hormone EPO, indulge in blood doping (injecting extra red blood cells), train at high altitude or sleep in a low-oxygen tent. Only the last two are allowed, of course, but the effect is the same. So the consequence of the ban on EPO and blood doping is to give an unfair advantage to athletes who can afford to train at altitude or invest in an altitude chamber—or on cunning doctors who can help them beat drug tests.

If we were really serious about making sport fair, we would try to ensure some sort of equality in the resources athletes have access to. And when genetics becomes advanced enough, we would introduce different divisions or some kind of handicapping system based on people's inherited advantages or disadvantages. After all, people who lack a Y chromosome already compete, separately from those who have one. Will it happen? Unlikely.

Steroids Can Be an Athlete's Tool

What many of us don't realize is that sports doping rarely gives you a free ride. If you or I were to take anabolic steroids and sit down in front of the telly, we would not build muscle or speed or endurance. Drugs allow you to train harder. They help you recover more quickly from a hard session so you can work hard again the next day. Some drugs boost the body's propensity for building muscle or its ability to use oxygen, but you still have to do the work.

Adrianne Blue, "It's the Real Dope," *New Statesman*, August 14, 2006.

Legalizing Steroids Can Make Their Use Safe

There is one decent argument against performance-enhancing drugs: safety. Many drugs taken by cheating athletes are dangerous, and allowing their use would force all athletes to take them to have any chance of winning. But the rules as they stand are clearly not designed with the safety of athletes in mind. A good example of this is the lack of any safety limit on the concentration of red blood cells, which beyond a certain level considerably increases the risk of heart attacks and strokes. Dehydration resulting from exercise makes matters even

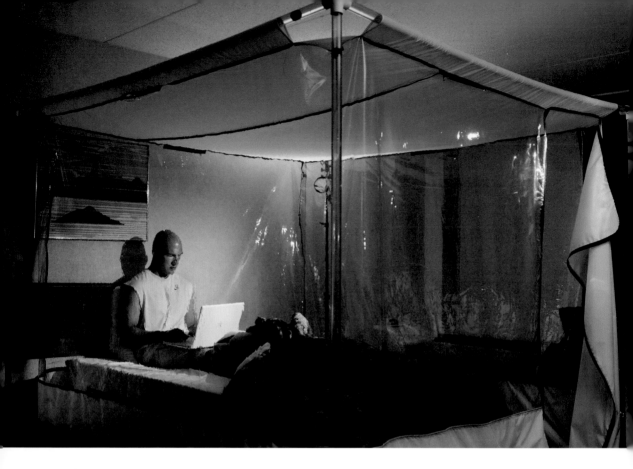

worse. Yet doping authorities allow athletes to compete no matter how high their blood cell concentration, as long as it is not due to doping. So it is fine for athletes to risk death, just as long as it is a natural death.

If those arguments do not convince you that we need to rethink the ban on drugs in sport, there is a more pragmatic one: the existing regime is not working. Clearly, many top athletes still resort to drugs. And the situation is only going to get worse. In the not too distant future, gene therapy could be used to boost the strength of muscles. The only way to detect such modifications may be to remove and test a piece of muscle. Are we really going to inflict that on athletes?

Switching Our Focus

There is another way: allow the use of drugs, and have sports authorities focus on testing the health of athletes rather than their use of drugs. This is the suggestion of ethicists Julian Savulescu at the University of Oxford and Bennett F'oddy at the University of Melbourne, Australia. They argue that any drugs that are safe should be permitted, whatever their effect on performance. Authorities would set a safe level for, say, red blood cell concentration, and anyone exceeding it would not be allowed to compete, whether their result was due to doping, altitude training or genetics.

Savulescu says he would prefer it if there were no drugs in sport. But the drugs are out there and they are not going to go away. So let's adopt the policy that is best for athletes and best for sport. We cannot live in fantasy land. Savulescu thinks doping authorities will have to adopt his idea sooner or later. Sooner would be better.

Analyze the essay:

1. Le Page closes his essay by citing the work of Julian Savulescu and Bennett F'oddy. Who are Savulescu and F'oddy, and why do you think Le Page chose to cite them in his essay? What do they lend his argument?

2. In this essay Le Page suggests that steroids should be legal because they make athletic competition more fair. How do you think the other authors featured in this section would respond to this suggestion? Write two or three sentences per author on what they would likely say to Le Page.

Students Should Be Tested for Steroids

Gregory Moore

In the following essay Gregory Moore argues that student athletes should be tested for steroids. He explains that steroids are frequently used by high school students as a result of trying to cope with pressure to perform well. Moore says that students who use steroids are mimicking the behavior of their favorite athletes—that is why it is so important that drug use at the professional level be curbed. Moore applauds officials in Texas for pushing forward legislation that would mandate drug testing of all students and encourages leaders in all states, and even the president, to do the same. He concludes that steroid use is too serious a problem to ignore and that drug testing can help reduce steroid use significantly.

Moore is the managing editor of the San Antonio Informer, a weekly newspaper for African Americans based in San Antonio, Texas.

Consider the following questions:

1. Why is it important for professional athletes to realize their actions have consequences, according to Moore?
2. What might have saved the life of Taylor Hooton, in the author's opinion?
3. Who is David Dewhurst, and what action has he taken toward mandating student drug testing, as reported by the author?

On July 24, 2004, I wrote an op/ed for the Black athlete Sports Network entitled, "In Lieu Of The BALCO Case, Are High School Athletes Still Trying To Mimic The

Gregory Moore, "Steroid Test at High School Level a Much Needed Tool," *American Chronicle*, May 29, 2007. Reproduced by permission.

Pros?" and I mentioned a young man by the name of Taylor Hooton. Hooton was a star baseball player in Plano, Texas but he was taking steroids and that ultimately ended his young life. His parents were distraught and the story was so compelling that it was on *60 Minutes II*. Since that story and since my op/ed, I've been a very strong proponent of high schools in Texas testing their young athletes for steroids and I was even more diligent once the BALCO[1] case emerged itself from the Bay Area and into our living rooms. So when it was announced by the University Interscholastic League [UIL] and the state legislature that an approved steroid test for high school athletes was finally here, not only did I applaud the decision, I was especially glad to see that lawmakers understood the dynamics of the situation at hand.

Fallout from the BALCO steroid scandal in California prompted the Texas state legislature and the University Interscholastic League to institute steroid tests for high school athletes.

1. BALCO stands for Bay Area Laboratory Cooperative, a company involved in a high-profile steroids scandal.

The Pressure for Students to "Juice"

Whether parents want to believe it or not, high school athletics is indeed big business; especially varsity football. Whether parents, students and/or faculty want to acknowledge this problem or not, steroid usage is indeed prevalent in [Texas] just like in any other state in the country and kids will mimic their professional athlete heroes. That is why it is so important for professional athletes to realize that their actions do indeed have consequences. It is why former players like Mark McGwire realize that just because androstenedione was a legal supplement for "him" to use when he was crushing Mickey Mantle's homerun record, he had an obligation to not have it sitting in his locker when cameras were interviewing him. That is why current pro athletes today need to be careful what

Americans Support Steroid Testing in Schools

A 2005 national poll found that the majority of Americans support testing student athletes for steroid use. Respondents said they believed testing was the best way to prevent steroid use in young athletes.

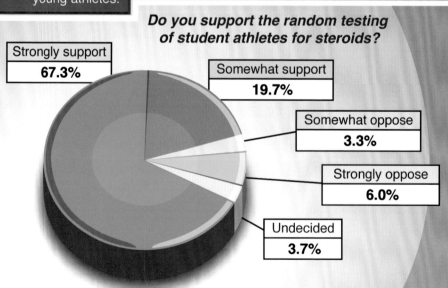

Do you support the random testing of student athletes for steroids?

Strongly support
67.3%

Somewhat support
19.7%

Somewhat oppose
3.3%

Strongly oppose
6.0%

Undecided
3.7%

Taken from: Sacred Heart University Polling Institute, April 20–28, 2005.

they say and what they use in their own workouts as again these younger athletes will run to the GNC store and try to score the EXACT same product that they see in a magazine or on television. And if a high school athlete is good enough to be an "elite" player, he or she will undoubtedly be subjected to the products that are available "under the table." Those products include steroids.

Testing Can Save Students' Lives

Parents who are thinking that this is singling out their athletes need to get a grip on the seriousness of this issue. If there was a procedure in place for the UIL in 2004, I firmly believe that the Hooton family would have young Taylor with them and that we may be reading about him in our favorite sports magazine. Hooton was that good of a baseball player from what I have gathered and that young man could have been something special for the Plano [Texas] area. So, from this perspective, every kid needs to be tested just so that there will be no tragedies like what the Hootons faced or the countless others that we may not even know about. What parents need to realize is that an athletic activity isn't a right their student athlete has had bestowed upon them but a privilege that is granted by the school itself. If a steroid test is administered and that parent or student does not want to subject him or herself to it, then they need to realize the gravity of their decision and the consequences that will ensue. There is no gray area here and there shouldn't be. Only the letter of the law needs to apply in this case so that everyone understands the seriousness of the situation and the importance of compliance by all involved.

> ## Clean Students Make Better Athletes
>
> The only way to get your arms around the problem of steroid use among athletes is to test them. . . . The benefit of testing high school athletes is that they'll learn not to use steroids at 16 or 17 rather than later—and colleges in turn will inherit clean students who are less apt to use drugs.
>
> Don Cook, quoted in "National Poll Reports 87.3% Support Random Steroid Testing Among High School Athletes," Sacred Heart University press release, May 2005. www.sacredheart.edu/pages/3375_may_2005.cfm.

Athletes' urine samples await testing at the UCLA Olympic lab. Proponents of testing say it will save lives.

So it is indeed a great honor to be a small foot soldier that has helped get this legislation to become a bill. Even though [Texas] Lt. Gov. David Dewhurst may not have read any of my columns, I know from e-mails over the past two years that somebody has been reading them on this topic and that somehow somebody thought that it was a worthwhile issue to pursue. For me, as one lone journalistic voice, I don't care who got this issue to become law, I'm just glad it became one. Across this country there are thousands of young men and women who are playing their selected sport without any incident of steroid use but there are those who will cheat. Those are the players who are bad for high school sports. If their parents support them in their use of illegal substances that enhance their abilities, then those parents are no good for the booster clubs either. Something had to be done and the Texas legislature has finally said it will.

All American Students Should Be Tested for Steroids

Lt. Gov. Dewhurst and other state legislatures in this state and across the country should be applauded for wanting to make it safe for our children to play high school sports. Parents should be clapping and getting behind these men and women who have bucked a status quo system and decided to put the safety of "our future" first and they left the partisan politics to a minimum. Other states have proposed similar laws and as great as this feat is today, much work is still needed to be accomplished for the future. There needs to be a national law that backs up the state's law as well. Maybe one day soon the elected officials at the Capitol and at 1600 Pennsylvania Avenue [the White House] will also put politics aside and help parents save their children from this silent killer.

Analyze the essay:

1. In the essay you just read, Gregory Moore uses examples and persuasive reasoning to make his argument that students should be tested for steroids. He does not, however, use any quotations to support his point. If you were to rewrite this article and insert quotations, what authorities might you quote from? Where would you place these quotes to bolster the points Moore makes?

2. Moore believes that drug testing students is the best way to curb steroid use in young athletes. How effective do you think drug testing can be? Does it actually prevent students from using drugs, and is it fair to do? If you agree, explain your reasoning. If you disagree, explain why and suggest an alternative to drug testing that might better reduce steroid use in students.

Students Should Not Be Tested for Steroids

Ty Meighan

In the following essay Ty Meighan argues against making steroid testing mandatory for student athletes. Meighan claims that testing is the wrong way to protect kids from drugs. For one, drug testing all students is a very costly endeavor—school budgets are already struggling—and Meighan believes schools will have to force taxpayers to shoulder the burden of the costs. Second, Meighan believes that steroid testing will not stop drug use in teens. He claims student athletes already know the dangers of steroid use and use them despite the risks. Finally, Meighan argues that testing is unnecessary because just a small percentage of student athletes use steroids, and that number shrinks every year. For all of these reasons, Meighan concludes that steroid testing is a waste of school resources and should not be made mandatory.

Meighan is editorial page editor of the *Standard-Times*, a newspaper in San Angelo, Texas, from which this essay was taken.

Consider the following questions:

1. How much would it cost taxpayers to pay for state-mandated steroid tests, as reported by the author?
2. What percentage of student athletes used steroids in 2004 and 2006, according to Meighan?
3. What does Meighan mean when he describes state-mandated steroid testing as a "good political issue?"

Ty Meighan, "Mandated Steroid Testing Wrong," *Standard-Times* (San Angelo, TX), March 13, 2007. Reproduced by permission.

With former Chicago Bear great Dick Butkus by his side, Texas Republican Lt. Gov. David Dewhurst last week rolled out a proposal for state-mandated random steroid testing of high school athletes in public schools.

The bill, which is sponsored by Sen. Kyle Janek, R-Houston, would require public school athletes to agree not to take steroids and submit to testing if randomly selected. Lawmakers hope to test as many as 22,000 students a year at 30 percent of the state's 1,300 high schools.

The legislation also requires all coaches from grades seven through 12 to complete an educational program regarding the health effects of steroid abuse.

Sounds like a great plan, huh? Who wouldn't support keeping kids off steroids?

High school students sign a pledge to stay drug-free during a rally in Chicago.

But before we get too caught up in the rhetoric of our elected officials, let's look at the facts.

Testing Is Expensive and Inappropriate

While I believe in protecting the health of all students, including athletes, state-mandated steroid testing is not the way to go.

Dewhurst's plan, which he first announced last year during his re-election campaign, raises many questions. It calls for the University Inter-scholastic League [UIL] to conduct and oversee the testing, as if the UIL didn't already have enough on its plate. The UIL is the governing body of high school sports and also oversees various academic competitions throughout the state.

Who will pay for the testing and how much will it cost? Estimates range from $2 million to $4 million a year. Will state budget-writers fund such a program? Should taxpayers even be paying for this testing?

Then there's the issue of local control. Why can't local schools govern steroid use through education campaigns and monitoring by coaches and parents? Conservatives, including Dewhurst, often tout local control but this plan requires more state meddling in an issue better handled by parents and local schools.

Students Will Take Steroids and Other Drugs Anyway

If we're concerned about students, why aren't lawmakers proposing random testing for other drugs, such as marijuana, heroin and cocaine? Studies have shown that abuse of illegal drugs and alcohol is more of a problem than steroid use in schools.

Mandatory Steroids Tests Hurt Students

Drug testing is expensive, taking away scarce dollars from other, more effective programs that keep young people out of trouble with drugs . . . [and] drug testing may drive students away from extra-curricular activities, which are a proven means of helping students stay out of trouble with drugs.

Jennifer Kern, Fatema Gunja, Alexandra Cox, Marsha Rosenbaum, Judith Appel, and Anjuli Verma, "Making Sense of Student Drug Testing: Why Educators Are Saying No," American Civil Liberties Union and the Drug Policy Alliance, January 2006. www.safety1st. org/images/stories/pdf/drugtesting.pdf.

Supporters of mandatory testing talk about the dangers of steroids. Duh. We all know steroids are dangerous and student-athletes should not take them. State law already prohibits the use and possession of steroids unless prescribed by a doctor.

Even so, most athletes who use steroids know they are endangering their health, but they believe the dangers are worth the risk.

Parents and Coaches Can Do More than Drug Tests

Parental and coach involvement is the key to this issue. I'll guarantee that parents who are paying attention to their children would be the first to know if they are taking steroids. Also, the facts show steroid abuse is not a

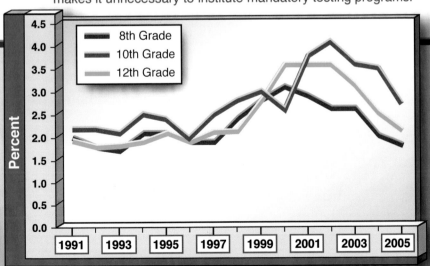

High School Student Steroid Use on the Decline

National data show steroid use among students continues to drop. Some experts say that the declining use of steroids makes it unnecessary to institute mandatory testing programs.

Taken from: *Monitoring the Future*; National Results on Adolescent Drug Use, 2005.

The author of this viewpoint believes that Texas lt. Gov. David Dewhurst's (pictured) mandate for random steroid testing in Texas high schools is too expensive to implement effectively.

major problem in high school sports, although Dewhurst claims otherwise.

"Steroid abuse is a real problem," he said. "Across Texas and the nation, young people are abusing steroids to become better athletes, but they have no idea how this substance can harm their bodies and minds."

Sure, Texas has had tragic cases where student-athletes have lost or ruined their lives with steroids, but we should base public policy decisions on facts, not political puffery.

Steroid Use Is Not a Major Problem Anyway

The fact is steroid use of student athletes is down from 2 percent in 2004 to 1.5 percent in 2006, according to a Texas A&M University study that surveyed more than 141,000 students in grades seven through 12. Studies have shown that alcohol, marijuana and cocaine are more of a concern than steroids, said Kim Rogers, a spokeswoman for UIL. A 2005 UIL survey of 1,184 schools in Texas found that most—868—believe the testing should be left up to local officials. Some schools are already testing and those that aren't say it is too expensive or steroids are not a problem on their campus, according to the survey.

It's clear steroid abuse is not the problem that some state officials claim. It is a good political issue because it looks as if our elected officials are doing something to protect students. A costly state-mandated testing program is the wrong approach and takes away much-needed funds from other programs.

If a public school campus has steroid problems, let local officials, parents and coaches find the appropriate solution.

Analyze the essay:

1. One of the reasons Meighan does not support mandatory steroid testing is that in his opinion, student steroid use is not that big of a problem. What evidence does he provide to support his claim that steroid use is not a serious problem among teens? Did you find it persuasive? Why or why not?

2. Meighan believes that parents and coaches should be responsible for solving the problem of student steroid use, not drug testing programs mandated by politicians. How do you think Gregory Moore, author of the previous viewpoint, would respond to this suggestion?

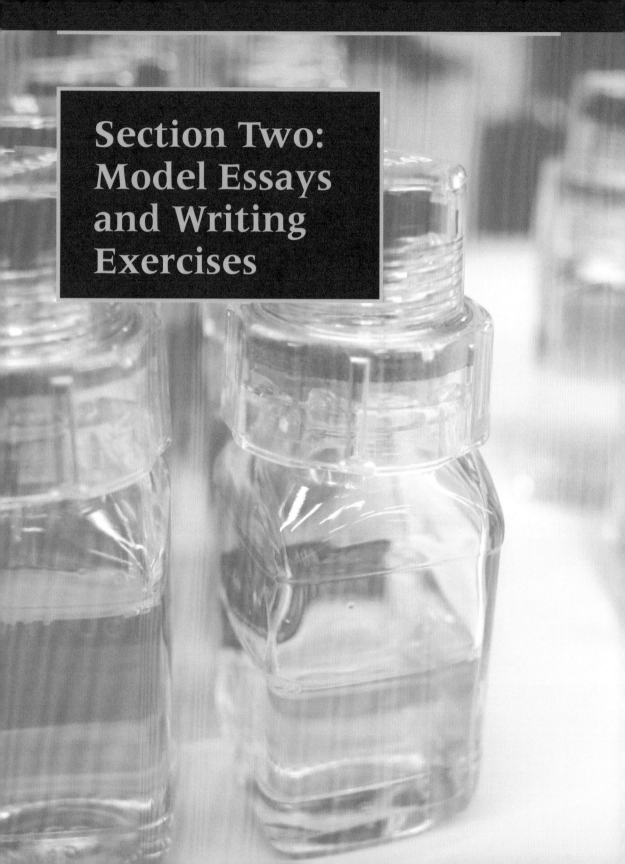

Section Two: Model Essays and Writing Exercises

The Five-Paragraph Essay

An *essay* is a short piece of writing that discusses or analyzes one topic. The five-paragraph essay is a form commonly used in school assignments and tests. Every five-paragraph essay begins with an *introduction,* ends with a *conclusion,* and features three *supporting paragraphs* in the middle.

The Thesis Statement. The introduction includes the essay's thesis statement. The thesis statement presents the argument or point the author is trying to make about the topic. The essays in this book all have different thesis statements because they are making different arguments about steroids.

The thesis statement should clearly tell the reader what the essay will be about. A focused thesis statement helps determine what will be in the essay; the subsequent paragraphs are spent developing and supporting its argument.

The Introduction. In addition to presenting the thesis statement, a well-written introductory paragraph captures the attention of the reader and explains why the topic being explored is important. It may provide the reader with background information on the subject matter or feature an anecdote that illustrates a point relevant to the topic. It could also present startling information that clarifies the point of the essay or put forth a contradictory position that the essay will refute. Further techniques for writing an introduction are found later in this section.

The Supporting Paragraphs. The introduction is then followed by three (or more) supporting paragraphs. These are the main body of the essay. Each paragraph presents and develops a *subtopic* that supports the essay's thesis statement. Each subtopic is spearheaded by a *topic sentence* and supported by its own facts, details, and examples. The writer can use various kinds of supporting material and details to back up the topic of each supporting paragraph. These may include statistics, quotations from people with special knowledge or expertise, historic facts, and anecdotes. A rule of writing is that specific and concrete examples are more convincing than vague, general, or unsupported assertions.

The Conclusion. The conclusion is the paragraph that closes the essay. Its function is to summarize or reiterate the main idea of the essay. It may recall an idea from the introduction or briefly examine the larger implications of the thesis. Because the conclusion is also the last chance a writer has to make an impression on the reader, it is important that it not simply repeat what has been presented elsewhere in the essay but close it in a clear, final, and memorable way.

Although the order of the essay's component paragraphs is important, they do not have to be written in the order presented here. Some writers like to decide on a thesis and write the introduction paragraph first. Other writers like to focus first on the body of the essay, and write the introduction and conclusion later.

Pitfalls to Avoid

When writing essays about controversial issues such as steroids, it is important to remember that disputes over the material are common precisely because there are many different perspectives. Remember to state your arguments in careful and measured terms. Evaluate your topic fairly—avoid overstating negative qualities of one perspective or understating positive qualities of another. Use examples, facts, and details to support any assertions you make.

The Descriptive Essay

T he previous section of this book provided you with samples of published persuasive writing on steroids. Many of these essays used description to convey their message. In this section, you will focus on developing your own descriptive writing skills.

A descriptive essay gives a reader a mental picture of the subject that the writer is exploring. Typically, descriptive writing uses the five senses—sight, sound, touch, taste, and smell—to help the reader experience what the writer has experienced. A descriptive writer carefully selects vivid examples and specific details to reveal people, places, processes, events, and ideas.

Using the Descriptive Essay

While an essay can be purely descriptive, descriptive papers written for the classroom are often persuasive or expository essays that use description to explain a memory, discuss an experience, or make a point. For example, in Viewpoint Four, Michael Le Page describes specific characteristics that make certain people extraordinarily gifted athletes. The specific details he includes—such as the possession of a genetic mutation called FPOK—having thin lower legs, and weighing on average 400 grams less than other athletes—give the reader concrete and vivid images and help the author drive home his argument.

Sometimes, descriptive essays are written in the first person (from the "I" point of view). Descriptive essays are a good format for the first person because details about a particular event or experience are well delivered through a person's memories, experiences, or opinions. In these cases, no one sentence can usually be singled out as the thesis statement. Instead, the essay has an *implied* thesis—a point of view made evident through the writer's careful use of details and examples. An example of first-person writing is found in Viewpoint Two by Donald M. Hooton. Hooton recounts how his son Taylor used steroids and as a result developed severe depression, which ultimately led him to take his own life. First-person writing is also displayed in Viewpoint Three, in which Douglas R. Hochstetler describes his experience as a sports ethics professor when arguing that steroid use makes sports unfair.

Descriptive Writing Techniques

An important element of descriptive writing is the use of images and specific and concrete details. Specific and concrete is the opposite of general and abstract. Descriptive writers should give their readers a fuller understanding of the topic by focusing on tangible details and by appealing to the five senses. See the accompanying box for examples of general nouns and their more specific variations.

General and Specific Descriptions

General	More specific	Most specific
drink	soda	root beer
dessert	pie	peach cobbler
car	station wagon	Pontiac Vibe
emotion	anger	fury
animal	bird	parrot

The use of *metaphors* and *similes* can also enliven descriptive writing. A *metaphor* is a word or phrase that compares two objects. A simile is a metaphor that includes the prepositions *like* or *as*. In Model Essay Two, "Steroids Are Never Worth It," the author uses a simile in Paragraph 4 to describe physical changes brought on by steroid use.

Some descriptive essays make use of *scene* and *exposition*. *The scene* is an element commonly found in fiction and in creative writing. With scene, a writer describes an event with moment-by-moment detail, often including dialogue if people are involved. With *exposition,* a writer explains, summarizes, or concisely recounts events that occur between scenes. Scene is comparable to "showing," while exposition is similar to "telling."

Tips to Remember

A descriptive essay should give the reader a clear impression of its subject. So, a writer must select the most relevant details. A few well-chosen details are more effective than dozens of random ones. You want the reader to visualize what you are describing but not feel overloaded with information. The room you are sitting in now, for example, is likely full of many concrete and specific items. To describe the room in writing, however, you would want to choose just a few of the most vivid details that would help convey your impression of and attitude about it.

A writer should also be aware of the kinds of words he or she uses in descriptive passages. Modifying words like adjectives and adverbs can enhance descriptive writing, but they should be used sparingly. Generally, verbs and nouns are more powerful than adjectives and adverbs. The overuse of modifying words makes the writing seem "wordy" and unnatural. Compare the phrases in the accompanying box to see the difference between wordy and concise language.

In the following section, you will read model descriptive essays about steroids and work on exercises that will help you write your own.

Wordy vs. Concise Language

Wordy	Concise
dirty animal with four legs and a tail	mangy mutt
a joyous festive occasion that will not be forgotten	a momentous event
he yelled out with all the force in his lungs	he screamed
she ate like she hadn't eaten in a hundred years	she devoured her meal

Athletes Who Use Steroids Should Have Their Records Deleted

Editor's Notes The first model essay argues that athletes who are caught using steroids should have their sports records deleted. The essay is structured as a five-paragraph descriptive essay in which each paragraph contributes a supporting piece of evidence to develop the argument. The author uses descriptive techniques to make her ideas specific and vivid; she also uses persuasive techniques to convince you of her argument.

The notes in the margin point out key features of the essay and will help you understand how the essay is organized. Also note that all sources are cited using Modern Language Association (MLA) style.* For more information on how to cite your sources see Appendix C. In addition, consider the following:

1. How does the introduction engage the reader's attention?
2. What descriptive techniques are used in the essay?
3. What purpose do the essay's quotes serve?
4. Does the essay convince you of its point?

■ Refers to thesis and topic sentences

■ Refers to supporting details

Paragraph 1

The essay opens with specific, descriptive details meant to grab your attention.

Americans despise cheaters. People who cut corners to reach a goal are typically viewed as weak, cowardly, and unethical. This is particularly true in sports—athletes who get caught throwing a game or rigging a score are publicly humiliated and sometimes even banished from their sport. Yet for some reason, there is debate over

---

* Editor's Note: In applying MLA style guidelines in this book, the following simplifications have been made: Parenthetical text citations are confined to direct quotations only; electronic source documentation in the Works Cited list omits date of access, page ranges, and some detailed facts of publication.

whether athletes who get caught using steroids should be able to keep their records and Hall of Fame accomplishments. Let's be honest: an athlete who uses steroids is no different than any other kind of cheater, and the sports community should recognize that by deleting the records of anyone caught using performance-enhancing drugs.

Paragraph 2

One reason why athletes should have their records deleted is because records that have been achieved with the aid of steroids unfairly trample on the records of the real athletes, the ones who used their natural ability to play the sport in the true spirit of the game. Indeed, steroids are nothing more than an illegal tool used to gain an unethical advantage over a competitor. It is deeply unfair for athletes who play by the rules to have their records obliterated by false ones set by cheaters. As one journalist put it when baseball star Barry Bonds's steroids-tainted record threatened to break the record of legend Hank Aaron: "Bonds cheated. Simple as that. Over the years, he pumped-up his 185-1b. body with illegal substances which transformed an above-average long-ball hitter to a 240-pound behemoth with a bat. But Aaron, a slim, 180-lb. marvel throughout his career, played by the rules. Instead of being celebrated, Bonds should be scorned." (Carter 10).

Paragraph 3

Another reason the records of steroids-using athletes should be deleted is because steroid use goes against everything we supposedly admire about athletes in the first place. Athletes are lauded as heroes because we respect their hard work, disciplined training, and their ability and willingness to stretch their minds and bodies to the limit. Douglas Hochstetler, who teaches a course on ethics in sports at Pennsylvania State University, has explained that Americans like sports precisely because they are fascinated with an athlete's ability to train, practice, and perform, not with his ability to take the most performance-enhancing drugs. Says Hochstetler, "We want to see which team has the best athletes and not the best engineers, geneticists, or chemists." In life in general,

This is the essay's thesis statement. It tells the reader what will be argued in the following paragraphs.

This is the topic sentence of paragraph 2. It is a subset of the essay's thesis. It tells what piece of the argument this paragraph will focus on.

What is the topic sentence of paragraph 3? Look for a sentence that tells generally what the paragraph's main point is.

This quote was taken from Viewpoint Three. When you see particularly striking quotes, save them to use to support points in your essays.

we have less respect for people who take shortcuts or cheat to reach their goal—sports are no exception.

Paragraph 4

This is the topic sentence of paragraph 4. It explores a different facet of the essay's thesis than the other paragraphs.

A final reason to wipe the records of steroids-using athletes is to deter athletes from using such drugs in the first place. When we give slap-on-the-wrist penalties to performance-enhancing drug users, we send the message that cheating with chemicals is not a serious infraction. With nothing at stake, there is no incentive for an athlete to reject steroids. Most Americans agree—which is why the majority of them support the deletion of drug-tainted records. According to a 2005 ABC/ESPN poll, 62 percent of Americans believe athletes who have been caught using steroids should not be allowed to keep their records, and 66 percent believe they should be banned from the Hall of Fame. That such a large majority of Americans believe it is inappropriate to celebrate tainted records is more proof that those records should be struck from the books.

This fact was taken from the visual that accompanies Viewpoint Three. Get in the habit of supporting your points with facts and statistics from credible sources—it lends legitimacy to your argument.

Paragraph 5

Note how the essay's conclusion wraps up the topic in a final, memorable way—without repeating the points made in the essay.

In the world of athletics, athletes are respected when they combine biological gifts with hard work to achieve success, not when they use unfair training techniques or get help from drugs and chemicals. If we want to delete steroids from athletics, we should start by deleting athletes' records that have been tainted by steroids use. Punishing those who disrespect their sport and their competitors is a fair and appropriate way to handle athletes who cheat by using steroids.

Works Cited

Carter, Richard. "Barry Bonds and Phony Sports Records Are for the Birds." *New York Amsterdam News* 28 Jun. 2007: 10.

Hochstetler, Douglas R. ". . . and Sport Shouldn't Be About Who Cheats Best." *Morning Call* [Allentown, PA] 18 Oct. 2007: A9.

Exercise 1A: Create an Outline from an Existing Essay

It often helps to create an outline of the five-paragraph essay before you write it. The outline can help you organize the information, arguments, and evidence you have gathered during your research.

For this exercise, create an outline that could have been used to write *Athletes Who Use Steroids Should Have Their Records Deleted*. This "reverse engineering" exercise is meant to help familiarize you with how outlines can help classify and arrange information.

To do this you will need to

1. articulate the essay's thesis
2. pinpoint important pieces of evidence
3. flag quotes that supported the essay's ideas, and
4. identify key points that supported the argument.

Part of the outline has already been started to give you an idea of the assignment.

Outline

I. Paragraph One
Write the essay's thesis:

II. Paragraph Two
Topic: Records that have been achieved with the aid of steroids unfairly trample on the records of the real athletes.

Supporting Detail i. The notion that it is deeply unfair for athletes who play by the rules to have their records obliterated by people who cheat.

Supporting Detail ii. Richard Carter quote: "Bonds cheated. Simple as that. Over the years, he pumped-up his 185-lb. body with illegal substances which transformed an above-average long-ball hitter to a 240-pound behemoth with a bat. But Aaron, a slim, 180-lb. marvel throughout his career, played by the rules. Instead of being celebrated, Bonds should be scorned."

III. Paragraph Three
Topic:

i. A description of why people regard athletes as heroes in the first place: because we respect their hard work, disciplined training, and their ability and willingness to stretch their minds and bodies to the limit.

ii.

IV. Paragraph Four
Topic: Making records-deletion a punishment for steroids use helps deter athletes from using drugs at all.

i.

ii.

V. Paragraph Five
i. Write the essay's conclusion:

Exercise 1B: Create an Outline for Your Own Essay

The first model essay expresses a particular point of view about steroids. For this exercise, your assignment is to find supporting ideas, choose specific and concrete details, create an outline, and ultimately write a five-paragraph essay making a different, or even opposing, point about steroids. Your goal is to use descriptive techniques to convince your reader.

Part I: Write a thesis statement.
The following thesis statement would be appropriate for an essay on why athletes who are caught using steroids should not have their records deleted:

Steroids are just a training tool that when used safely help athletes do exactly what the public wants them to do: perform spectacular athletic feats.

Or, see the sample paper topics suggested in Appendix D for more ideas.

Part II: Brainstorm pieces of supporting evidence.

Using information found in this book and from your own research, write down three arguments or pieces of evidence that support the thesis statement you selected. Then, for each of these three arguments, write down supportive facts, examples, and details that support it. These could be

- statistical information;
- personal memories and anecdotes;
- quotes from experts, peers, or family members;
- observations of people's actions and behaviors;
- specific and concrete details.

Supporting pieces of evidence for the above sample thesis statement include:

- The idea that there is a "level playing field" in athletics is debunked when one considers that many athletes are endowed with almost superhuman traits—particularly large feet; a gene that produces more red blood cells; a protein that helps build a particular kind of muscle fiber—that give them a distinct advantage over other athletes.
- Training at high altitude and being able to afford expensive athletic equipment are other ways in which athletes gain unfair advantages over one another.
- Quote by Michael Le Page in Viewpoint Four: "There is a way to level the playing field: allow athletes to make up for their natural disadvantages by taking performance-enhancing drugs."

Part III: Place the information from Part I in outline form.

Part IV: Write the arguments or supporting statements in paragraph form.

By now you have three arguments that support the essay's thesis statement, as well as supporting material. Use the outline to write out your three supporting arguments in paragraph form. Make sure each paragraph has a topic sentence that states the paragraph's thesis clearly and broadly. Then, add supporting sentences that express the facts, quotes, details, and examples that support the paragraph's argument. The paragraph may also have a concluding or summary sentence.

Steroids Are Never Worth It

Essays drawn from memories or personal experiences are called personal narratives. The following essay is this type of essay. It is not based on research or the retelling of someone else's experiences, such as other descriptive essays you have read in this book. Instead, this essay consists of an autobiographical story that recounts memories of an event that happened to someone involving steroids.

The essay differs from the first model essay in that it is written in the subjective or first-person ("I") point of view. Writing in the first person is a powerful way to deliver stories and make points. Also, many colleges require a first-person essay as part of their application process. Therefore, becoming familiar with the first person will broaden your ability as a writer and make your college application powerful and memorable.

As you did for the first model essay, take note of the essay's components and how they are organized (the sidebars in the margins will help you identify the essay's pieces and their purpose).

Refers to thesis and topic sentences

Refers to supporting details

Paragraph 1

Today's student athletes face tremendous pressure to be endlessly bigger, faster, and stronger—I should know, I'm one of them. The pressure to be the best can really get to a person sometimes, and there are some of us who will do anything—even take steroids—to be as good as they think their parents and coaches want them to be. But after watching my friend's disastrous experiment with steroids, I can confidently say that messing with steroids just to win a few games is totally not worth it.

Even personal narratives can have thesis statements. This thesis statement tells you what this essay will discuss.

Paragraph 2

I learned this important lesson just before my junior year of high school, when everyone at my school who played a sport was nervous about whether they would make

What details are used to make the story come alive for the reader? Do you find that they make the story more realistic and interesting?

the varsity teams or be stuck for another year on junior varsity. My friend Jason and I were on the wrestling team together, and coach had repeatedly told us we were some of the best players in the whole school, maybe even the county. He said if we could bulk up over the summer and work out to increase our size and strength, he would definitely have a place for us on varsity.

Paragraph 3

Determined to make the varsity team, Jason and I hit the gym hard every day for the first three weeks of summer. I felt a little stronger, but knew I still had a long way to go before I was varsity material. But one day, Jason's impatience got the better of him: he announced he had a plan, a way for us to get big enough in time for team selection later in the summer. A guy he knew had started taking a steroid called Anadrol and could get it for us pretty easily. I told Jason there was no way I would take it—I had heard steroids can do really gross stuff to your body—and I just didn't want to win that badly.

The author uses a *simile* to describe the effects of steroids on his friend's body. For more on similes and other descriptive techniques see Preface B.

Paragraph 4

But Jason figured there was no way he would make varsity without some chemical help. So he started taking the Anadrol, and within just a few weeks he looked amazing—his back, arms, shoulders, and legs were so muscular he looked like a rippling Adonis. At first I was jealous and kicking myself for not starting the steroids cycle with him. But not long after he was selected for the varsity team, I noticed some odd changes in Jason. He developed a severe puffy, bloated look and began suffering from debilitating headaches that were at times so bad he couldn't even go outside into direct sunlight. Plus, he became really moody and at times would be so irritable you could barely say hello to him without having it escalate into an argument.

"Plus" is a transitional phrase. It keeps the sentences linked together and keeps ideas moving. Make a list of all the transitional phrases that appear in this essay.

Paragraph 5

The rapid change in Jason's physical appearance, coupled with his extreme headaches, bloating, and irritability, quickly aroused suspicions at school. Coach confronted

Jason, and eventually got it out of him that he had been using steroids. Not only was Jason banned from all athletic events and suspended for two weeks, he was humiliated. People in school were calling him Juiced Up Jason, and someone painted "Roid Rager" in red paint all over his car. Though the immediate bloating and headache side effects went away after Jason stopped taking steroids, I learned later that Anadrol can cause serious, sometimes life-threatening liver problems including cysts, tumors, or liver failure. Jason may have done permanent damage to his organs, which could cause catastrophic problems for him later in life. But even though Jason is in bad shape, I know that his experiment with steroids could have been even worse—he could have met the same fate of Taylor Hooton, a sixteen-year-old baseball player who committed suicide after suffering from severe depression brought on by steroid use. Watching my friend's steroid spiral taught me that no matter what team, game, or title is at stake, steroid use is always dangerous and never worth it.

These specific, descriptive details help you get a sense of Jason's experience. Always use specific rather than vague details when writing.

The author uses the example of Taylor Hooton, whose death is described in more detail in Viewpoint Two of this book.

Exercise 2A: Examining Introductions and Conclusions

Whether an essay is a first-person account, a report on an event, or a formal persuasive paper, all pieces of writing feature introductory and concluding paragraphs that are used to frame the main ideas being presented. Along with presenting the essay's thesis statement, well-written introductions should grab the attention of the reader and make clear why the topic being explored is important. The conclusion reiterates the essay's thesis and is also the last chance for the writer to make an impression on the reader. Strong introductions and conclusions can greatly enhance an essay's effect on an audience.

The Introduction

Several techniques can be used to craft an introductory paragraph. An essay can start with

- an anecdote: a brief story that illustrates a point relevant to the topic;
- startling information: facts or statistics that elucidate the point of the essay;
- setting up and knocking down a position: a position or claim believed by proponents of one side of a controversy, followed by statements that challenge that claim;
- historical perspective: an example of the way things used to be that leads into a discussion of how or why things work differently now;
- summary information: general introductory information about the topic that feeds into the essay's thesis statement.

Problem One

Reread the introductory paragraphs of the model essays and of the viewpoints in Section One. Identify which of the techniques described above are used in the example essays. How do they grab the attention of the reader? Are their thesis statements clearly presented?

Problem Two

Write an introduction for the essay you have outlined and partially written in Exercise 1B using one of the techniques described above.

The Conclusion

The conclusion brings the essay to a close by summarizing or returning to its main ideas. Good conclusions, however, go beyond simply repeating these ideas. Strong conclusions explore a topic's broader implications and reiterate why it is important to consider. They may frame the essay by returning to an anecdote featured in the opening paragraph. Or, they may close with a quotation or refer back to an event in the essay. In opinionated essays, the conclusion can reiterate which side the essay is taking or ask the reader to reconsider a previously held position on the subject.

Problem Three

Reread the concluding paragraphs of the model essays and of the viewpoints in Section One. Which were most effective in driving their arguments home to the reader? What sorts of techniques were used to do this? Did these paragraphs appeal emotionally to the reader or bookend an idea or event referenced elsewhere in the essay?

Problem Four

Write a conclusion for the essay you have outlined and partially written in Exercise 1B using one of the techniques described above.

Exercise 2B: Using Quotations to Enliven Your Essay

No essay is complete without quotations. Get in the habit of using quotes to support at least some of the ideas in your essays. Quotes do not need to appear in every paragraph, but often enough so that the essay contains voices aside from your own. When you write, use quotations to accomplish the following:

- Provide expert advice that you are not necessarily in the position to know about.
- Cite lively or passionate passages.
- Include a particularly well-written point that gets to the heart of the matter.
- Supply statistics or facts that have been derived from someone's research.
- Deliver anecdotes that illustrate the point you are trying to make.
- Express first-person testimony.

Problem One
Reread the essays presented in all sections of this book and find at least one example of each of the above quotation types.

Important things to remember when using quotations:

- Note your sources' qualifications and biases. This way your reader can identify the person you have quoted and can put their words in a context.
- Put any quoted material within proper quotation marks. Failing to attribute quotes to their authors constitutes plagiarism—an author taking someone else's words or ideas and presenting them as his or her own. Plagiarism is a very serious infraction and must be avoided at all costs.

Students Protest Against Mandatory Steroids Testing

Editor's Notes The third model essay discusses steroids using a different aspect of the descriptive essay. It reports on a student-led effort to ban mandatory steroids testing in their Texas high school. It uses descriptive techniques to capture the details of the effort, helping the students' efforts come alive for the reader. To do this, the author conducted an interview with the organizer of the effort, Dwayne Lapadis, and also interviewed people who attended an anti-steroids-testing rally. The information gleaned during the course of the interviews allowed the author to get inside information, details, and opinions on the event. Because they yield these types of details, interviews can be a useful tool when writing a descriptive essay. More information about conducting an interview is found in Exercise 3A and 3B that follow the essay.

Also, unlike the previous model essays, the following essay is more than five paragraphs. Sometimes five paragraphs are simply not enough to adequately develop an idea. Extending the length of an essay can allow the reader to explore a topic in more depth or present multiple pieces of evidence that together provide a complete picture of a topic. Longer essays can also help readers discover the complexity of a subject by examining a topic beyond its superficial exterior. Moreover, the ability to write a sustained research or position paper is a valuable skill you will need as you advance academically.

Refers to thesis and topic sentences

Refers to supporting details

Paragraph 1

"We love you, and we don't want to lose you." So said President George W. Bush in his 2004 State of the Union speech, in which he called on America's teachers, parents, and coaches to get tough on steroid use in high schools. Since then, some states have passed laws that require all student athletes to submit to steroids tests. In Texas, this program is slated to begin in 2008, and by June 2009 state officials expect to have tested as many as fifty thousand student athletes for steroids. But many students, parents, and privacy groups such as the ACLU have opposed mandatory steroids testing on the grounds that it is an invasion of privacy, a waste of school funds, and unnecessary because just a small portion of American students have a steroids problem. Given these issues, in 2008 a group of motivated students at an Austin, Texas, high school started a grassroots effort to oppose mandatory steroids testing of student athletes at their school. According to sixteen-year-old Dwayne Lapadis who led the effort to organize the ban, "There are a lot of problems with mandating steroids testing for high school students—and a bunch of us wanted to do something about it."

How does the introductory paragraph set the stage for the event the author is reporting on?

Paragraph 2

Lapadis was moved to organize the effort to ban mandatory steroids testing after researching the issue for a project in his debate class. He came to the conclusion that the cost-benefit ratio of steroids testing—that is, the amount of good an act does versus the amount it costs—is very low, and therefore not worth it. "Right now, it costs our school about $65 to test each student," said Lapadis. "We would love to see that money put towards new computers or athletic equipment—something that is going to positively enhance our school." Furthermore, Lapadis and his supporters believe that because only a few students have ever experimented with steroids, mandatory testing is unnecessary and inappropriate. Explained Lapadis, "National polls show that the minority of high school students have tried steroids once in their lifetimes, let alone use it on a regular basis. In 2007, the National Institute on Drug Abuse reported that only about 2 percent of 12th graders, 1.8 percent of 10th graders, and 1.5 percent of 8th graders had ever tried

Make a list of all transitional phrases used in the essay.

These are the same statistics that appear in Appendix A of this book. Lapadis did research on his topic and used credible information to support his argument.

steroids. Two percent! That's an incredibly tiny number to justify the costs and privacy invasions of mandatory steroids testing."

Paragraph 3

Lapadis decided he wanted to organize an effort to prevent steroids testing from becoming mandatory at his school, so he decided to form a group dedicated to resisting the new law. He got permission from his class adviser to start a group, which he called SAMST—Students Against Mandatory Steroids Testing. As per school policy, he needed a teacher to sponsor the group. After finding one, he hung flyers around school asking for fellow classmates who felt passionately about the issue to join. Ultimately, about fifteen students came to his first meeting, which was on a Wednesday afternoon. "You might think that the only people who joined were athletes," said Lapadis, "but it was a total mix of all different types of students— the common thread was that we all think steroids testing is a bad idea."

This is Paragraph 3's topic sentence. Note how it broadly states what will be covered in the paragraph.

Paragraph 4

At the group's first meeting, they articulated their goal: to convince their community that their school should not comply with state law that would soon make steroids testing mandatory. They debated ways to make this goal a reality: Ideas included publishing articles on the issue in the school newspaper, circulating a petition among the student body, and creating a Web site about the group's effort. After coming up with these ideas, they broke into subgroups to do research on the issue and dole out responsibilities: students who excelled at writing were placed in charge of writing op-eds for the student paper; those who were technologically savvy were tasked with creating a Web site and blogging on the issue; and the social butterflies of the group were put in charge of circulating a petition, with the goal of getting as many signatures as possible.

What specific details are discussed in Paragraph 4?

But the group's overriding goal was to hold a community-wide rally that could raise awareness for their issue and convince the community to join their effort. After doing research to support their side of the issue, writing persuasive articles on the topic and circulating a petition (on which they collected more than five hundred signatures, about 45 percent of the student body), the SAMST students did just that—they held an Against Mandatory Steroids Testing rally in the school's quad. First, they obtained permission from school authorities to hold the event. This included getting the appropriate signatures on permissions forms, making sure the quad was not otherwise occupied on the day they wanted to hold the rally, and coordinating with the school's custodial and technology teams about renting tables, chairs, podiums, projectors, laptops, and other equipment. Said Blanca Rios, one of the founding members of SAMST, "I never realized how much time and effort goes into planning big events like this. It's seriously a full-time job!"

On the day of the rally, the SAMST students set up booths at which students could get information on why mandatory steroids testing should be banned at their school. Each booth was organized by topic. For example, one booth went into detail about the testing process to demonstrate how an individual's privacy could be violated. It described how the proposed testing measures would work: students would not be told they were being tested until testing officials arrived on campus and pulled them from class. They would then be escorted to the bathroom by a same-sex test monitor and asked to urinate into a collection cup. Athletes would also be required to empty their pockets, remove bulky clothing, and lift their shirts to prove they were not hiding anything in their waistband. To drive home their point, the students set up a simulated testing scenario and went so far as to have a SAMST member dress up like a testing officer and frisk visitors who visited

What descriptive details are found in paragraph 6? What specific information is provided?

the booth, asking them to please step aside and provide a urine sample. Said one athlete, "It was totally embarrassing! I definitely understand now why people think mandatory steroids testing is a privacy issue—it wasn't clear to me before but having a tester ask me to pee in front of people definitely drove home the point!"

Which of the paragraph's points does this quote serve to support?

Paragraph 7

Midway through the rally, Lapadis, Rios, and other SAMST members gave brief speeches about why they had organized the event and what they hoped to gain from it: "We are not condoning the use of steroids," said Rios in her speech. "Rather, we support the use of comprehensive drug education in fighting steroids use among young people, rather than forcing them to submit to expensive, invasive, and unnecessary drug tests." To reinforce the group's opposition to steroid use, Lapadis talked about the physical side effects from using steroids, which he said include hair loss, mental illness, liver damage, infertility, and many others. During his speech, images flashed on a screen behind him that showed sickening pictures of bodybuilders on steroids, their muscles unnaturally pumped up and distorted.

What is the topic sentence of paragraph 7? How did you recognize it?

These descriptions are meant to convey the scene to the reader in a unique and powerful way.

Paragraph 8

The rally to ban mandatory steroids testing was met with mixed reviews by those who attended. Some supported the efforts and said the information they were presented with helped them make up their minds about which side of the issue they were on. Said one student, "I hadn't given much thought to the issue before, but the leaflets I read and the speeches I heard made me think twice. It does kind of seem like our school's money could be better spent in other places." Said another, "I've never heard of anyone at our school doing steroids, so it seems like a lot of fuss for a problem that affects a super low percentage of the student body." As proof that the SAMST rally succeeded in convincing people to support the effort to ban mandatory steroids testing, an additional 328 signatures were added to the group's petition.

These comments lend the essay a personal feel. Make sure to integrate unique and interesting quotes from those you interview in your reports.

Paragraph 9

But not everyone who attended was persuaded to join the group's cause. "Steroids testing seems like a small price to pay to make sure our athletes are playing by the rules and not doing anything stupid just for the sake of winning a game," said one coach. A teacher who attended the rally held a similar view: "Steroids are very dangerous drugs, so I support all efforts to keep young people from using them. However, the fact that these students organized and rallied around an issue they cared about is very impressive and should be both commended and encouraged."

Paragraph 10

The SAMST rally to ban mandatory steroids testing was attended by more than eight hundred students, teachers, parents, and administrators, demonstrating at the very least that interest in the issue was high. Whether they believed that mandatory steroids testing should be banned or not, all who attended the rally agreed that the information presented gave them a lot to think about. Ultimately, the students were not able to override their state's law mandating steroids testing, but they did succeed in getting a lot of people to carefully consider what was at stake in the controversy. "We got the information out there to the community, and that's the best we can do," said Lapadis. For more information on the issue of mandatory steroids testing, check out the National Center for Drug Free Sport, on the Web at www.drugfreesport.com.

Works Cited

Bush, George W. "State of the Union Address." 20 Jan. 2004 < www.whitehouse.gov/news/releases/2004/ 01/20040120-7.html > .

Friedman, Lauri S. Personal interviews. 24 Apr. 2008.

Exercise 3A: Conduct an Interview

Essay Three, *Students Protest Against Mandatory Steroids Testing,* was written after conducting interviews with Dwayne Lapadis, Blanca Rios, and several other people. When reporting on events that occur in your community, you will probably need to interview people to get critical information and opinions. Interviews allow you to get the story behind a participant's experiences, enabling you to provide a fuller picture of the event.

The key to a successful interview is asking the right questions. You want the respondent to answer in as much detail as possible so you can write an accurate, colorful, and interesting piece. Therefore, you should have a clear idea of what general pieces of information you want to find out from the respondent before you begin interviewing. The six classic journalist questions—who, what, when, where, why, and how—are an excellent place to begin. If you get answers to each of these questions, you will end up with a pretty good picture of the event that took place.

There are many ways to conduct an interview, but the following suggestions will help you get started:

Step One: Choose a setting with little distraction.

Avoid bright lights or loud noises, and make sure the person you are interviewing feels comfortable speaking to you. Professional settings such as offices, places of business, and homes are always appropriate settings for an interview. If it is a phone interview, be sure you can clearly hear what the person is saying (so do not conduct the interview on a cell phone while walking on a busy city block, for example).

Step Two: Explain who you are and what you intend to learn from the interview.

Identify yourself. For what publication are you writing? If you are writing for a school paper, identify the paper. If you are conducting research for an ongoing project, explain the project's goals and in what way you expect the interviewee can help you reach them. Indicate how long you expect the interview to take, and get all contact information up front.

Step Three: Ask specific questions, and start at the beginning.

Make sure you ask at least two questions that address each of the following ideas: who, what, where, when, why, and how. Who was involved in the event? What happened during the course of the event? Where did it take place? Specific questions will change depending on what type of event you are covering. Follow your instincts; if you do not know something or have a question, ask. The answer will likely yield good information that will enhance your report.

Step Four: Take notes.

Never rely on your memory when conducting an interview. Either type or jot down notes or ask permission to tape or otherwise record the interview.

Step Five: Verify quotes and information.

Before you write your report, it is important to go back to your source to double-check key points of information. Also, you must run any quotes you intend to use by the source before you put them in your report. This is to make sure you heard the person accurately and are not misrepresenting their position.

Types of Questions to Ask During an Interview

Questions you will ask your interviewee tend to fall into a few basic categories.

Knowledge—what they know about the topic or event. This can include historical background, logistics, and outcomes of an event. For example, Blanca Rios in Essay Three provided the interviewer with information about the process of planning a community-wide rally.

Sensory—ask questions about what people have seen, touched, heard, tasted or smelled. These details will help your readers vividly imagine the event you are reporting on.

Behavior—what motivated the person to become involved in this project or movement? What do they hope to gain by having their story publicized?

Opinions, values, and feelings—what the person thinks about the topic or event. These questions result in opinionated or personal statements that you, as an objective reporter, most likely will not make in your report. For example, in Essay Three the author quotes from rally participants to express opinions on the event in a way that would be inappropriate for an objective reporter to do.

Exercise 3B: Report on an Event

Reports show up in many publications—newspapers, magazines, journals, Web logs (blogs) are just some of the places people read about events and activities under way in their community. Think about the type of event you would like to report on. It could be a trip summary; the happenings of a local or school event, such as a parade, speech, assembly, or rally; a sports game; a party; or another experience in which people are coming together to get something done. Think next about the type of publication in which your report would best appear. Trip summaries, or travelogues, make great fodder for blogs; reports on school events such as sports games or performances are best featured in the school paper.

Before you report on an event, make sure you have done thorough research. Look over all notes from your interviews. Outline a road map for your essay to follow (see exercises in this book on how to outline an essay prior to writing it). Examine where quotations, information, and other details will fit best. After you absorb and organize all the information you have collected, you are ready to write.

News reports tend to be objective, so make sure your writing style is impartial and matter-of-fact. Also, be sure to provide the reader with enough information to visualize the event, but not so much that you bombard them with unnecessary or unrelated details. Use the other writing exercises found in this book—on using quotations, writing introductions and conclusions, and gathering research—to help you write the report. Then submit it for publication!

Write Your Own Descriptive Five-Paragraph Essay

Using the information from this book, write your own five-paragraph descriptive essay that deals with steroids. You can use the resources in this book for information about issues relating to this topic and how to structure this type of essay.

The following steps are suggestions on how to get started.

Step One: Choose your topic

The first step is to decide what topic to write your descriptive essay on. Is there any subject that particularly fascinates you about steroids? Is there an issue you strongly support, or feel strongly against? Is there a topic you feel personally connected to or one that you would like to learn more about? Ask yourself such questions before selecting your essay topic. Refer to Appendix D: Sample Essay Topics if you need help selecting a topic.

Step Two: Write down questions and answers about the topic.

Before you begin writing, you will need to think carefully about what ideas your essay will contain. This is a process known as *brainstorming*. Brainstorming involves asking yourself questions and coming up with ideas to discuss in your essay. Possible questions that will help you with the brainstorming process include:

- Why is this topic important?
- Why should people be interested in this topic?
- How can I make this essay interesting to the reader?
- What question am I going to address in this paragraph or essay?
- What facts, ideas, or quotes can I use to support the answer to my question?

Questions especially for descriptive essays include:

- Have I chosen a compelling story to examine?
- Have I used vivid details?
- Have I made scenes come alive for my reader?

- What qualities do my characters have? Are they interesting?
- Does my descriptive essay have a clear beginning, middle, and end?
- Does my essay evoke a particular emotion or response from the reader?

Step Three: Gather facts, ideas, and anecdotes related to your topic. This book contains several places to find information about issues relating to steroids, including the viewpoints and the appendices. In addition, you may want to research the books, articles, and Web sites listed in Section Three, or do additional research in your local library. You can also conduct interviews if you know someone who has a compelling story that would fit well in your essay.

Step Four: Develop a workable thesis statement. Use what you have written down in steps two and three to help you articulate the main point or argument you want to make in your essay. It should be expressed in a clear sentence and make an arguable or supportable point.

Example:

All of America's student athletes should be required to pass a steroids test before they are allowed to play. This could be the thesis statement of a descriptive essay that argues that student testing for steroids should be mandatory. Supporting paragraphs would explore reasons why the author thinks this and include specific details of the effects of steroids on the human body and details of steroids testing programs.

Step Five: Write an outline or diagram.
1. Write the thesis statement at the top of the outline.
2. Write roman numerals I, II, and III on the left side of the page with A, B, and C under each numeral.
3. Next to each roman numeral, write down the best ideas you came up with in step three. These should all directly relate to and support the thesis statement.

4. Next to each letter write down information that supports that particular idea.

Step Six: Write the three supporting paragraphs.

Use your outline to write the three supporting paragraphs. Write down the main idea of each paragraph in sentence form. Do the same thing for the supporting points of information. Each sentence should support the paragraph of the topic. Be sure you have relevant and interesting details, facts, and quotes. Use transitions when you move from idea to idea to keep the text fluid and smooth. Sometimes, although not always, paragraphs can include a concluding or summary sentence that restates the paragraph's argument.

Step Seven: Write the introduction and conclusion.

See Exercise 2A for information on writing introductions and conclusions.

Step Eight: Read and rewrite.

As you read, check your essay for the following:

- ✔ Does the essay maintain a consistent tone?
- ✔ Do all paragraphs reinforce your general thesis?
- ✔ Do all paragraphs flow from one to the other? Do you need to add transition words or phrases?
- ✔ Have you quoted from reliable, authoritative, and interesting sources?
- ✔ Is there a sense of progression throughout the essay?
- ✔ Does the essay get bogged down in too much detail or irrelevant material?
- ✔ Does your introduction grab the reader's attention?
- ✔ Does your conclusion reflect back on any previously discussed material, or give the essay a sense of closure?
- ✔ Are there any spelling or grammatical errors?

Section Three: Supporting Research Material

Facts About Steroids

Editor's Note: These facts can be used in reports to reinforce or add credibility when making important points.

- Anabolic steroids were developed in the late 1930s to treat hypogonadism, a condition in which the testes do not produce sufficient testosterone for normal growth, development, and sexual functioning.
- Steroids are still used by doctors to treat delayed puberty, some types of impotence, and wasting of the body caused by HIV infection or other diseases.
- During the 1930s scientists discovered that a particular class of steroids, called anabolic steroids, could help grow muscle in laboratory animals. This led to the use and abuse of these drugs first by bodybuilders and weight lifters, and next by athletes in other sports.
- The Anabolic Steroids Control Act of 1990 placed anabolic steroids into Schedule III of the Controlled Substances Act (CSA). As a result, anabolic steroids are defined as any drug or hormonal substance chemically and pharmacologically related to testosterone (other than estrogens, progestins, and corticosteroids) that promotes muscle growth.
- For a first offense, possession of illegal anabolic steroids carries a maximum penalty of one year in prison and a minimum $1,000 fine.
- The maximum penalty for a first offense of trafficking illegal steroids is five years in prison and a fine of $250,000.
- The maximum period of imprisonment and the maximum fine both double if it is an individual's second offense.
- Street names for steroids include Roids, Juice, Candy, Pumpers, Stackers, Balls or Bulls, Weight Trainers, Arnies, Arnolds, A's or Anabolics.

Steroids are taken either as a pill or an oral liquid, or are injected. Brand names of steroids include:

- Anadrol® (oxymetholone)
- Oxandrin® (oxandrolone)
- Dianabol® (methandrostenolone)
- Winstrol® (stanozolol)
- Deca-Durabolin® (nandrolone decanoate)
- Durabolin® (nandrolone phenylpropionate)
- Depo-Testosterone® (testosterone cypionate)
- Equipoise® (boldenone undecylenate) (veterinary product)

Steroids are used in patterns called *cycling*, which involves taking steroids for a specific period of time, stopping use, and then starting again.

Some users combine different types of steroids in a process known as stacking.

Some users slowly escalate steroid use and then gradually taper the dose in a process known as pyramiding.

The 2007 Monitoring the Future Study, which surveys students in eighth, tenth, and twelfth grades, found that:

- 1.5 percent of eighth graders have used steroids at least once in their lifetimes.
- 1.8 percent of tenth graders have used steroids at least once in their lifetimes.
- 2.2 percent of twelfth graders have used steroids at least once in their lifetimes.
- 0.8 percent of eighth graders have used steroids at least once in the past year.
- 1.1 percent of tenth graders have used steroids at least once in the past year.
- 1.4 percent of twelfth graders have used steroids at least once in the past year.
- 0.4 percent of eighth graders have used steroids at least once in the past month.
- 0.5 percent of tenth graders have used steroids at least once in the past month.

- 1.0 percent of twelfth graders have used steroids at least once in the past month.

Regarding the ease with which students can obtain steroids, the 2007 Monitoring the Future Study found that:

- 17.0 percent of eighth graders said that steroids were "fairly easy" or "very easy" to obtain.
- 27.7 percent of tenth graders said that steroids were "fairly easy" or "very easy" to obtain.
- 40.1 percent of twelfth graders said that steroids were "fairly easy" or "very easy" to obtain.
- 57.4 percent of twelfth graders said they considered using steroids to be a "great risk."

According to the National Institute on Drug Abuse, steroid use among high school students has increased more than 67 percent since 1991.

Side Effects of Steroids

The side effects of steroids in both males and females include:

- High blood cholesterol levels
- Cardiovascular problems
- Severe acne
- Thinning of hair and baldness
- Fluid retention
- High blood pressure
- Liver disorders (including liver damage and jaundice, a yellowing of the skin)
- Risk of contracting HIV and other blood-borne diseases from sharing infected needles
- Sexual and reproductive disorders
- Atrophy (wasting away) of the testicles
- Loss of sex drive
- Diminished or decreased sperm production
- Breast and prostate enlargement in males
- Decreased hormone levels
- Sterility in males

- Menstrual irregularities
- Infertility in females
- Negative fetal development during pregnancy
- Masculinizing effects in women, such as facial hair, diminished breast size, permanently deepened voice, and enlargement of the clitoris
- Mood swings
- Impaired judgment
- Depression
- Nervousness
- Extreme irritability
- Delusions
- Hostility and aggression

Steroid Testing

A 2005 poll by the Sacred Heart University Polling Institute found:

- 87 percent of Americans support random testing of high school athletes for steroid use.
- 67.3 percent said they "strongly support" such testing; 19.7 percent said they "somewhat support" such testing.
- 9.3 percent said they were opposed to random testing of high school athletes for steroid use.
- 3.3 said they were "somewhat opposed" while 6 percent said they were "strongly opposed."
- 3.7 percent were undecided.

According to the National Federation of State High School Associations' survey of athletic directors, in 2005 less than 4 percent of the nation's high schools tested for steroids use.

To test high school students for steroids costs $50–$100 per test.

According to *USA Today,* as of 2007, state laws regarding steroids testing in schools were as follows:

States that mandate steroids testing:

- Florida—law states that 1 percent of athletes in football, baseball, and weightlifting must be tested.

- New Jersey—first state to pass a steroid testing law.
- Texas—law mandates widespread testing.

States in which laws regarding steroids exist, but testing is not mandatory:

- California—it is illegal for high school athletes to take ephedra and other performance-enhancing supplements.
- Iowa—athletes may be suspended for steroid use, but state law prohibits random drug testing.
- Louisiana—laws allow students to participate in surveys about extent of steroid use.
- Maine—school systems are required to address steroids in their drug and alcohol policies.
- Michigan—school boards are required to have an established policy on steroids.
- Minnesota—selling performance-enhancing drugs to minors is punishable with a maximum twenty-year prison sentence.
- Pennsylvania—school boards are required to enforce rules that prohibit steroid use, but stops short of testing students for steroids.
- Virginia—an athlete can be banned from sports for two years if his or her principal and superintendent determine steroids have been used.

States with local or regional steroid-related policy:

- Alaska—the largest school district in Anchorage has a policy banning steroid use.
- Georgia—athletics association has policy statement denouncing use of steroids.
- Massachusetts—activities association has wellness program with regulations against steroid use.
- Mississippi—a number of schools have mandatory testing programs.
- Missouri—steroids and other drug testing became mandatory in the Francis Howell School District in 2006.

- Nevada—athletes must sign a contract saying they will not use alcohol or drugs, including steroids.
- North Dakota—rules call for penalties for steroid use, but no testing.
- Oklahoma—several school districts have mandatory testing policies.
- Oregon—the athletic association ruled in favor of educating about the dangers of steroids versus testing for them, saying that the state's extensive education program can reach fifteen students for the cost of one steroid test.
- Rhode Island—athletics association has policy statement denouncing use of steroids.
- Wisconsin—athletics association provides schools with DVDs and literature on steroids.
- West Virginia—Logan County schools test up to 2 percent of athletes each week.
- Wyoming—Campbell County High School in Gillette tests for steroids.

Finding and Using Sources of Information

No matter what type of essay you are writing, it is necessary to find information to support your point of view. You can use sources such as books, magazine articles, newspaper articles, and online articles.

Using Books and Articles

You can find books and articles in a library by using the library's computer or cataloging system. If you are not sure how to use these resources, ask a librarian to help you. You can also use a computer to find many magazine articles and other articles written specifically for the Internet.

You are likely to find a lot more information than you can possibly use in your essay, so your first task is to narrow it down to what is likely to be most usable. Look at book and article titles. Look at book chapter titles, and examine the book's index to see if it contains information on the specific topic you want to write about. (For example, if you want to write about steroids testing in high schools and you find a book about drug testing in general, check the chapter titles and index to be sure it contains information about steroids testing specifically before you bother to check out the book.)

For a five-paragraph essay, you do not need a great deal of supporting information, so quickly try to narrow down your materials to a few good books and magazines or Internet articles. You do not need dozens. You might even find that one or two good books or articles contain all the information you need.

You probably do not have time to read an entire book, so find the chapters or sections that relate to your topic, and skim these. When you find useful information, copy it onto a note card or notebook. You should look for supporting facts, statistics, quotations, and examples.

Using the Internet

When you select your supporting information, it is important that you evaluate its source. This is especially important with information you find on the Internet. Because nearly anyone can put information on the Internet, there is as much bad information as good information. Before using Internet information—or any information—try to determine if the source seems to be reliable. Is the author or Internet site sponsored by a legitimate organization? Is it from a government source? Does the author have any special knowledge or training relating to the topic you are looking up? Does the article give any indication of where its information comes from?

Using Your Supporting Information

When you use supporting information from a book, article, interview, or other source, there are three important things to remember:

1. *Make it clear whether you are using a direct quotation or a paraphrase.* If you copy information directly from your source, you are quoting it. You must put quotation marks around the information and tell where the information comes from. If you put the information in your own words, you are paraphrasing it.

Here is an example of a using a quotation:

Commentator Gregory Moore believes that professional athletes need to realize that when they do steroids, they influence countless numbers of high school students to follow in their footsteps. As Moore writes, "Kids will mimic their professional athlete heroes. That is why it is so important for professional athletes to realize that their actions do indeed have consequences."

Here is an example of a brief paraphrase of the same passage:

Commentator Gregory Moore believes that professional athletes need to realize that when they do steroids, they influence countless numbers of high school students to follow in their footsteps. Moore warns that young people look up to and imitate athletic heroes, making it important for the pros to realize that when they do steroids, it's not just a personal decision.

2. *Use the information fairly.* Be careful to use supporting information in the way the author intended it. For example, it is unfair to quote an author as saying, "Steroids are great drugs," when he or she intended to say, "Steroids are great drugs for treating certain illnesses such as autoimmune disease, but when taken recreationally can have grave consequences." This is called taking information out of context. This is using supporting evidence unfairly.

3. *Give credit where credit is due.* Giving credit is known as citing. You must use citations when you use someone else's information, but not every piece of supporting information needs a citation.
   - If the supporting information is general knowledge—that is, it can be found in many sources—you do not have to cite your source.
   - If you directly quote a source, you must cite it.
   - If you paraphrase information from a specific source, you must cite it.

If you do not use citations where you should, you are *plagiarizing*—or stealing—someone else's work.

Citing Your Sources
There are a number of ways to cite your sources. Your teacher will probably want you to do it in one of three ways:
   - Informal: As in the example in number 1 above, tell where you got the information as you present it in the text of your essay.
   - Informal list: At the end of your essay, place an unnumbered list of all the sources you used. This

tells the reader where, in general, your information came from.

- Formal: Use numbered footnotes or endnotes. Footnotes or endnotes are generally placed at the end of an article or essay, although they may be placed elsewhere depending on your teacher's requirements.

Works Cited

Moore, Gregory. "Steroid Test at High School Level a Much Needed Tool." *American Chronicle* 29 May 2007.

Using MLA Style to Create a Works Cited List

You will probably need to create a list of works cited for your paper. These include materials that you quoted from, relied heavily on, or consulted to write your paper. There are several different ways to structure these references. The following examples are based on Modern Language Association (MLA) style, one of the major citation styles used by writers.

Book Entries

For most book entries you will need the author's name, the book's title, where it was published, what company published it, and the year it was published. This information is usually found on the inside of the book. Variations on book entries include the following:

A book by a single author:
> Simon, Jonathan. *Governing Through Crime: How the War on Crime Transformed American Democracy and Created a Culture of Fear.* New York: Oxford University Press, 2007.

Two or more books by the same author:
> Mernissi, Fatima. *Beyond the Veil.* San Francisco: Saqi, 2003.
> ———. *Fear of the Modern World.* New York: Basic Books, 2002.

A book by two or more authors:
> Esposito, John L., and Dalia Mogahed. *Who Speaks for Islam? What a Billion Muslims Really Think.* Washington, DC: Gallup, 2008.

A book with an editor:
> Friedman, Lauri S., ed. *Writing the Critical Essay: Democracy.* Farmington Hills, MI: Greenhaven, 2008.

Periodical and Newspaper Entries

Entries for sources found in periodicals and newspapers are cited a bit differently than books. For one, these sources usually have a title and a publication name. They also may have specific dates and page numbers. Unlike book entries, you do not need to list where newspapers or periodicals are published or what company publishes them.

An article from a periodical:
> Bauer, Henry H. "The Mystery of HIV/AIDS." *Quadrant* Jul.–Aug. 2006: 61–64.

An unsigned article from a periodical:
> "The Chinese Disease? The Rapid Spread of Syphilis in China." *Global Agenda* 14 Jan. 2007.

An article from a newspaper:
> Bradsher, Keith. "A New, Global Oil Quandary: Costly Fuel Means Costly Calories." *New York Times* 19 Jan. 2008: A2.

Internet Sources

To document a source you found online, try to provide as much information on it as possible, including the author's name, the title of the document, date of publication or of last revision, the URL, and your date of access.

A Web source:
> Butts, Jeffrey. "Too Many Youths Facing Adult Justice." 25 Aug. 2004 Urban Institute. 7 May 2008. < www.urban.org/publications/900728.html >.

Your teacher will tell you exactly how information should be cited in your essay. Generally, the very least information needed is the original author's name and the name of the article or other publication.

Be sure you know exactly what information your teacher requires before you start looking for your supporting information so that you know what information to include with your notes.

Sample Essay Topics

Steroid Use in Professional Sports Is a Serious Problem

Steroid Use in Professional Sports Is Not a Serious Problem

Teen Steroid Abuse Is a Serious Problem

Teen Steroid Abuse Is Not a Serious Problem

Performance-Enhancing Drugs Should Be Illegal

Performance-Enhancing Drugs Should Be Legal

Performance-Enhancing Drugs Violate the Spirit of the Game

Performance-Enhancing Drugs Make for More Entertaining Games

Athletes Cheat When They Use Steroids

Steroid Use Is Not Cheating

Athletes Who Use Steroids Should Have Their Records Deleted

Athletes Who Use Steroids Should Not Have Their Records Deleted

Student Athletes Should Be Drug Tested for Steroids

Student Athletes Should Not Be Drug Tested for Steroids

Drug Testing Reduces Steroid Use in Student Athletes

Drug Testing Does Not Reduce Steroid Use in Student Athletes

A Comprehensive Education Program Can Reduce Steroid Use Among Student Athletes

Harsher Penalties Are Needed for Athletes Who Use Steroids

There Should Be No Penalties for Athletes Who Use Steroids

The War on Drugs Reduces Steroid Abuse

The War on Drugs Does Not Reduce Steroid Abuse

Legalizing Steroids Would Reduce Drug Abuse

Legalizing Steroids Would Increase Drug Abuse

Topics for Descriptive Essays

The Effects of Steroids on a User

The Ins and Outs of a Steroid-Testing Program

The Problem of Steroids in Professional Sports

Different Types of Steroids and How They Work in the Body

The Difference Between Anabolic Steroids and Corticosteroids

Organizations to Contact

American College of Sports Medicine
PO Box 1440, Indianapolis, IN 46206-1440
(317) 637-9200 • Web site: www.acsm.org

This organization is a good source of information on the risks of performance-enhancing drugs such as steroids and human growth hormone.

American Council for Drug Education (ACDE)
164 W. Seventy-fourth St., New York, NY 10023
(800) 488-DRUG • e-mail: acde@phoenixhouse.org
Web site: www.acde.org

The American Council for Drug Education informs the public about the harmful effects of abusing drugs and alcohol, including steroids. It offers the public access to scientifically based, compelling prevention programs and materials.

Cato Institute
1000 Massachusetts Ave. NW, Washington, DC 20001-5403
(202) 842-0200 • e-mail: service@cato.org
Web site: www.cato.org

The institute is a public policy research foundation dedicated to limiting the control of government and to protecting individual liberty. Cato, which strongly favors drug legalization, publishes the *Cato Journal* three times a year and the *Cato Policy Report* bimonthly.

Drug Enforcement Administration (DEA)
2401 Jefferson Davis Hwy., Alexandria, VA 22301
(202) 307-1000 • Web site: www.dea.gov

The DEA is the federal agency charged with enforcing the nation's drug laws. The agency concentrates on stopping the smuggling and distribution of narcotics in the United States and abroad. It publishes the *Drug Enforcement Magazine* three times a year.

The Drug Policy Alliance

70 W. Thirty-sixth St., 16th Flr., New York, NY 10018
(212) 613-8020 • e-mail: dc@drugpolicy.org
Web site: www.dpf.org/homepage.cfm

The Drug Policy Alliance is the leading organization in the United States promoting alternatives to the war on drugs. The alliance supports the creation of drug policies that respect individual rights, protect community health, and minimize the involvement of the criminal justice system.

The Drug Reform Coordination Network

1623 Connecticut Ave. NW, 3rd Flr.,
Washington, DC 20009
(202) 293-8340 • e-mail: drcnet@drcnet.org
Web site: http://stopthedrugwar.org

The Drug Reform Coordination Network opposes the "War on Drugs" and works for drug policy reform from a variety of perspectives, including harm reduction, reform of sentencing and forfeiture laws, medicalization of marijuana, and the promotion of an open debate on drug prohibition.

International Amateur Athletics
Federations (IAFF)

17 Rue Princesse Florestine, BP 359 MC98007, Monaco
(377) 9310-8888 • Web site: www.iaaf.org

The IAFF is the international governing body of athletics, with 180 member federations around the world. It produces its own list of doping control regulations and distributes an antidrug booklet for young athletes. Its Web site has a whole section devoted to antidoping efforts.

Join Together

One Appleton St., 4th Flr., Boston, MA 02116-5223
(617) 437-1500 • e-mail: info@jointogether.org
Web site: www.jointogether.org

Founded in 1991, Join Together supports community-based efforts to reduce, prevent, and treat substance abuse. It publishes community action kits to facilitate grassroots efforts to increase awareness of substance abuse issues as well as a quarterly newsletter.

National Center on Addiction and Substance Abuse at Columbia University (CASA)
633 Third Ave., 19th Flr., New York, NY 10017-6706
(212) 841-5200 • Web site: www.casacolumbia.org

CASA is a private nonprofit organization that works to educate the public about the costs and hazards of substance abuse and the prevention and treatment of all forms of chemical dependency, including steroids. The center supports treatment as the best way to reduce drug addiction.

National Clearinghouse for Alcohol and Drug Information
PO Box 2345, Rockville, MD 20847-2345
(800) 729-6686 • e-mail: shs@health.org • Web site: www. health.org

The clearinghouse distributes publications of the U.S. Department of Health and Human Services, the National Institute on Drug Abuse, and other federal agencies concerned with alcohol and drug abuse.

National Collegiate Athletic Association (NCAA)
700 W. Washington St., PO Box 6222, Indianapolis, IN 46206-6222
(317) 917-6222 • Web site: www.ncaa.org

The NCAA is the national administrative body overseeing all intercollegiate athletics. It publishes up-to-date information on regulations (including those concerning performance-enhancing drugs) for college athletes in the United States.

National High School Athletic Coaches Association (NHSACA)
PO Box 10065, Fargo, ND 58196
e-mail: office@hscoaches.org
Web site: www.hscoaches.org

The NHSACA seeks to promote cooperation among coaches, school administrators, the press, and the public. It holds seminars in sports medicine and promotes educational programs on drug abuse awareness.

National Institute on Drug Abuse (NIDA)

6001 Executive Blvd., Room 5213 MSC9561, Bethesda, MD 20892-9561

(301) 443-6245 • e-mail: information@nida.nih.gov

Web site: www.nida.nih.gov

NIDA supports and conducts research on drug abuse—including funding the yearly *Monitoring the Future Survey*—to improve addiction prevention, treatment, and policy efforts. It has undertaken extensive surveys on steroid use in American high schools. Survey information and more is available on NIDA's Web site.

National Scholastic Anti-Doping Program (NSADP)

8730 Big Bend Blvd., St. Louis, MO 63119

(314) 963-3404 • Web site: www.nsadp.com

The NSADP was created to develop a complete steroid educational package and testing program. It employs certified antidoping officers to conduct testing, a certified Medical Review Officer (MRO) to review all test results, and cutting-edge computer technology to assure confidentiality and accuracy of all testing data. The NSADP works directly with the UCLA Olympic Testing Lab, the only World Anti-Doping Association (WADA)–certified laboratory in the United States.

Office of National Drug Control Policy

PO Box 6000, Rockville, MD 20849-6000

(800) 666-3332 • e-mail: ondcp@ncjrs.org

Web site: www.whitehousedrugpolicy.gov

The Office of National Drug Control Policy is responsible for formulating the government's national drug strategy and the president's antidrug policy as well as coordinating the federal agencies responsible for stopping drug trafficking. Drug policy studies are available upon request.

Partnership for a Drug-Free America
405 Lexington Ave., Ste. 1601, New York, NY 10174
(212) 922-1560 • Web site: www.drugfreeamerica.org

The Partnership for a Drug-Free America is a nonprofit organization that utilizes media communication to reduce demand for illicit drugs in America. Best known for its national antidrug advertising campaign, the partnership works to "unsell" drugs to children and to prevent drug use among kids.

U.S. Olympic Committee (USOC)
One Olympic Plaza, Colorado Springs, CO 80909
(719) 632-5551 • Web site: www.usoc.org

Like other national Olympic committees around the world, the USOC publishes codes of ethics to which Olympic athletes are expected to adhere. The USOC also has compiled a detailed list of drugs athletes are banned from using in competition.

Bibliography

Books

Assael, Shaun, *Steroid Nation: Juiced Home Run Totals, Anti-aging Miracles, and a Hercules in Every High School: The Secret History of America's True Drug Addiction.* New York: ESPN Books, 2007.

Bailes, Julian, *When Winning Costs Too Much: Steroids, Supplements, and Scandal in Today's Sports World.* Lanham, MD: Taylor, 2005.

Egendorf, Laura K., *Performance-Enhancing Drugs.* San Diego: ReferencePoint, 2007.

Ezra, David, "Asterisk: Home Runs, Steroids, and the Rush to Judgment." Chicago: Triumph, 2008.

Fainaru-Wada, Mark, and Lance Williams, *Game of Shadows: Barry Bonds, BALCO, and the Steroids Scandal That Rocked Professional Sports.* New York: Gotham, 2006.

Jendrick, Nathan, *Dunks, Doubles, Doping: How Steroids Are Killing American Athletics.* Guilford, CT: Lyons, 2006.

Johnson, David, *Falling Off the Thin Blue Line: A Badge, a Syringe, and a Struggle with Steroid Addiction.* Lincoln, NE: iUniverse, 2007.

Kiesbye, Stefan, ed., Contemporary Issues Companion: *Steroids.* Detroit: Greenhaven, 2007.

Lenehan, Patrick, *Anabolic Steroids.* New York: Taylor & Francis, 2003.

Walker, Ida, *Illicit and Misused Drugs: Steroids: Pumped Up and Dangerous.* Broomall, PA: Mason Crest, 2007.

Periodicals

Arrison, Sonia, "Enhancing the Quest for Gold," *Boston Globe,* February 26, 2006. www.boston.com/news/globe/editorial_opinion/oped/articles/2006/02/26/enhancing_the_ quest_for_gold.

Baumbach, Jim, "Steroids Testing in High Schools Long Overdue," *Newsday.com*, May 24, 2007. www.news day.com/sports/highschool/ny-spjim0524,0,4304728. column.

Blue, Adrianne, "It's the Real Dope," *New Statesman*, August 14, 2006.

Carter, Al, "Face It: We Love Cheaters in Sports," *San Antonio Express-News*, February 17, 2008.

Carter, Richard, "Barry Bonds and Phony Sports Records Are for the Birds," *New York Amsterdam News*, June 28, 2007.

Celizic, Mike, "Time for Steroid Testing in High School: If Kids Can't Get Caught, the Problem Will Only Get Worse," MSNBC.com, April 24, 2004. www.msnbc.msn. com/id/4556250.

DuPont, Robert, interviewed by Margot Adler, "Does Drug Testing Student Athletes Deter Drug Abuse?" National Public Radio, August 21, 2006. www.justicetalking.org/ transcripts/060821_drugsstudents_transcript.pdf.

Goldberg, Linn, "Steroids in Sports: Cheating the System and Gambling Your Health," testimony before the U.S. House of Representatives Subcommittee on Commerce, Trade, and Consumer Protection & Subcommittee on Health, March 10, 2005. http://energycommerce.house. gov/reparchives/108/Hearings/03102005hearing1452/ Goldberg.pdf.

Hardin, Ed, "We've Lost Our Way, and Our Heroes Cheat," *Greensboro* (NC) *News Record*, January 16, 2008.

Jendrick, Nathan, "Let's Get the Drug Testing Job Done," *TimedFinals.com*, October 29, 2007. www.timedfinals. com/29102007/in-my-mind-lets-get-the-drug-testing-job-done.

Kayser, Bengt, Alexandre Mauron, and Andy Miah, "Legalisation of Performance-Enhancing Drugs," *Lancet*, December 17, 2005.

Kern, Jennifer, "Negatives of Drug Testing," National Federation of State High School Associations, 2007. www.nfhs.org/web/2007/12/pointcounterpoint_drug_testing.aspx.

Kern, Jennifer, Fatema Gunja, Alexandra Cox, Marsha Rosenbaum, Judith Appel, and Anjuli Verma, "Making Sense of Student Drug Testing: Why Educators Are Saying No," American Civil Liberties Union and the Drug Policy Alliance, January 2006. www.safety1st.org/images/stories/pdf/drugtesting.pdf.

Knight, John R., and Sharon Levy, "The National Debate on Drug Testing in Schools," *Journal of Adolescent Health*, vol. 41, no. 5, November 2007.

Le Page, Michael, "Only Drugs Can Stop the Sports Cheats," *New Scientist*, August 19, 2006.

McCarthy, Colman, "Barry Bonds Is Just Like the Rest of Us," *National Catholic Reporter*, August 31, 2007.

McCormick, Patrick, "It's How You Play the Game," *U.S. Catholic*, vol. 71, no. 11, November 2006.

Mitchell, George J., "Report to the Commissioner of Baseball of an Independent Investigation into the Illegal Use of Steroids and Other Performance Enhancing Substances by Players in Major League Baseball," December 13, 2007. http://files.mlb.com/summary.pdf.

Mitten, Matthew J., "Is Drug Testing of Athletes Necessary?" *USA Today Magazine*, vol. 134, no. 2726, November 2005.

Nelson, Hillary, "Natural-Born Cheaters; Steroids Might Be the Least of Our Troubles," *Concord* (NH) *Monitor*, February 17, 2008.

Pinsent, Matthew, "My Drugs Test Confirms IOC Must Bulk Up to Win Fight Against Cheats," *Times* (London), February 20, 2008.

Robinson, Eugene, "We Want Superman Athletes," *Buffalo News*, December 19, 2007. www.buffalonews.com/248/story/232405.html.

Saltzman, Marissa, "Chemical Edge: The Risks of Performance-Enhancing Drugs," *Odyssey,* May 2006.

Souhan, Jim, "Outing a Cheat Is Best Form of Justice," *McClatchy-Tribune News Service,* November 15, 2007.

Sullum, Jacob, "Bush on Steroids: Why Must Sports Be Drug-Free?" *Reason,* January 23, 2004. www.reason.com/news/show/35605.html.

Svare, Bruce B., "What Athletic Directors Can Do About the Steroid Abuse Crisis," *Coach & Athletic Director,* vol. 75, no. 9, April 2006.

Vecsey, George, "Scamming for Dollars: It's Time to Get Angry About Athletes Who Cheat," *International Herald Tribune,* October 8, 2007.

Weiner, Robert, "Field of Play," *Honolulu Star Bulletin,* November 29, 2007. http://starbulletin.com/2007/11/29/editorial/commentary.html.

Zedalis, Joe, "Steroid Testing Hits Home at High Schools," Rivals.com, 2008. http://highschool.rivals.com/content.asp?CID = 741122.

Web Sites

Anabolic Steroid Abuse Page (www.steroidabuse.gov). This page of the National Institute for Drug Abuse's Web site is dedicated to providing information specifically about steroids.

Baseball's Steroid Era (www.baseballssteroidera.com). Contains news, lists, time lines, statistics, and quotes regarding professional athletes whose steroid use has been discovered.

The National Center for Drug-Free Sport (www.drugfreesport.com/index.asp). A national entity that focuses on the specific needs of sports organizations. Has an entire section devoted to issues relating to steroid use.

Squeezing Out the Juice: Tackling the Steroid Issue (http://ncadi.samhsa.gov/multimedia/webcasts/w.

aspx?ID = 453). This is an hour-long Webcast that examines the health effects of steroids and how the pressure to win influences choices people make. Includes information on what the Drug Enforcement Administration (DEA), legislators, sports leagues, and schools are doing about performance-enhancing drugs.

Steroids Drug Addiction and Abuse (www.narconon.ca/steroids.htm). This page deals with substance abuse issues related to steroids.

World Anti-Doping Agency (WADA) (www.wada-ama.org/en). The mission of WADA is to promote and coordinate at an international level the fight against doping in sports in all forms. Its Web site includes reports, news, and statistics about antidoping efforts around the globe.

Index

Students
  should be tested for
    steroids, 40–45
  should not be tested for
    steroids, 46–51
  See also High school
    athletes
Suicide, 20–21
Sullum, Jacob, 8, 10,
  15

T
Thorpe, Ian, 35
Tour de France, 28

U
University
  Interscholastic League
  (IUL), 41, 48

V
Varsity football, 42

W
Warning signs, 25
Woods, Tiger, 8
World Anti-Doping
  Agency, 35

Picture Credits

About the Editor

Lauri S. Friedman earned her bachelor's degree in religion and political science from Vassar College in Poughkeepsie, NY. Her studies there focused on political Islam. Friedman has worked as a nonfiction writer, a newspaper journalist, and an editor for more than 8 years. She has accumulated extensive experience in both academic and professional settings.

Friedman is the founder of LSF Editorial, a writing and editing outfit in San Diego. Her clients include Greenhaven Press, for whom she has edited and authored numerous publications on controversial social issues such as gay marriage, prisons, genetically modified food, racism, suicide bombers, and drug abuse. Every book in the *Writing the Critical Essay* series has been under her direction or editorship, and she has personally written more than eighteen titles in the series. She was instrumental in the creation of the series, and played a critical role in its conception and development.